Fashion Design Essentials

ROCKPORT

Text © 2011 by Rockport Publishers
Design © 2011 by Rockport Publishers

First published in the United States of America in 2011 by
Rockport Publishers, a member of
Quayside Publishing Group
100 Cummings Center
Suite 406-L
Beverly, Massachusetts 01915-6101
Telephone: (978) 282-9590
Fax: (978) 283-2742
www.rockpub.com

10 9 8 7 6 5 4 3 2 1

ISBN-13: 978-1-59253-701-3
ISBN-10: 1-59253-701-4

Digital edition published in 2011
eISBN-13: 978-1-61058-043-4

Library of Congress Cataloging-in-Publication Data available

Design: Kathie Alexander
Photographs and illustrations by Jay Calderin unless otherwise noted.

Printed in China

Fashion Design Essentials

100 Principles of Fashion Design

BEVERLY MASSACHJSETTS

ROCKPORT PUBLISHERS

Jay Calderin

CONTENTS

Creative ideas are elevated by experience and expertise. This book sets forth a challenge to fashion designers: Continue to expand your horizons, hone your skills, and experiment with strategies. The idea behind collecting and cataloging the essential principles of fashion design is to build a framework for artful examination that the designer can revisit regularly for inspiration and instruction. This book is for anyone devoted to fashion—whether you are a professional designer, a design student, or a fashion DIY enthusiast.

The world of fashion design is constantly changing—what was in style last month may be old hat now, but if you know how to stay ahead of trends and keep your design skills sharp, you'll always be ahead of the curve. *Fashion Design Essentials* offers principles, tools, and processes for succeeding in all fashion endeavors.

Editing the list to one hundred concepts is meant to help organize and prioritize this information for maximum efficiency. The references in each layout have been selected because they hone in on the essence of the topic with precision, while allowing for diverse reinterpretation, not simply reproduction.

Five primary areas of investigation provide the structure for the book. In many ways, they can be described as a set of best practices for cultivating creativity:

Thought
Intellectual exercises that are intended to serve as catalysts for channeling creativity

Inventory
Definitions and applications for using or repurposing tools, manpower, and raw materials for fashion design

Technique
Fundamental skills for identifying and executing fashion design ideas

Artistry
Creative rituals that help conjure and cultivate the imaginative instincts of a fashion designer

Navigation
Diverse strategies designed to allow a fashion designer to negotiate a clear path to success

Each essential concept is ultimately a source of stimuli that must be deciphered and then shaped to fit the project at hand. Dedication and attention to detail during that examination will help leverage a designer's vision.

In an attempt to round out the whole experience, some philosophical debates are woven into the ideas throughout the book, such as the benefits or far-reaching impact today's fashion designers will have on the foreseeable future.

Pierre Cardin coat and hat,
Autumn/Winter 1959/60

1 Historical Reference and Reverence

It is said that those who don't learn from history are doomed to repeat it. Within the frame of fashion, those who don't learn from history are doomed to waste a wealth of inspiration. Three mainstays in the fashion world that are restyled time and again are corsets, aprons, and kimonos.

The corset, originally a foundation garment, still reigns supreme on the fashion landscape. Commonly associated with goth, fetish, and most recently, Steampunk fashions, couturiers such as Thierry Mugler and Jean Paul Gaultier have been responsible for raising the corset to an iconic status.

The apron at its most functional protects clothing from wear and tear. Aprons at their most glamorous have graced the runways of Alexander McQueen, Miu Miu, and Marc Jacobs as fashion accessories. Short-waist aprons made in practical fabrics as well as decorative hostess aprons speak to a time when homemaking was a way of life for most women. Long versions such as the bistro apron are among many that are used in the service industry. The bib-style apron can take shape in leather, rubber, or heavy canvas for more rugged uses. The pinafore is a decorative style of apron that conjures up images of life on the prairie—a look that was very popular in the 1970s. The cobbler apron is a pullover style with a front, a back, and ties on the side. Whether it is incorporated into a collection by way of nostalgia or utility, the apron still makes strides in fashion.

The kimono is a full-length, T-shaped robe. When part of a traditional ensemble, it is secured with an obi sash. The kimono is made from a tan, which is a fixed bolt of fabric measuring 14 inches by 12.5 yards (35 cm x 12 m). The length is cut into four panels of fabric that make up the two sides of the body and both sleeves. A collar and lapel-style panels are added with small strips of fabric. Kimonos were originally disassembled for cleaning and reconstructed by hand.

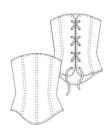

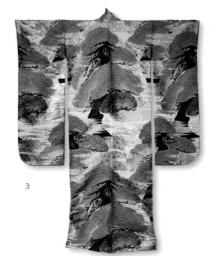
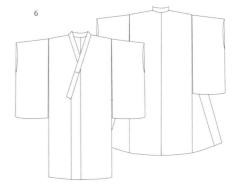

1. **Corset** by Joe Carl

2. **Vintage apron**—Poor Little Rich Girl

3. **"Old Japan" Bridal Kimono** (circa 1980s)

4. **Corset**

5. **Apron**

6. **Kimono**

French model Audrey Marnay in a tweed corset suit by Thierry Mugler, haute couture collection, Autumn/Winter 1998/99

2 Emulation and Innovation

Emulating styles from the past often will go a long way in fashion design, as everything eventually makes a comeback. The grace of Grecian gowns forever immortalized in stone is a prime example of the power of a fashion idea that does not simply survive, but thrives in the imaginations of fashion designers throughout history. In the 1920s, Madeleine Vionnet was influenced by the dances of Isadora Duncan who, in turn, was inspired by Greek sculptures. While Vionnet commanded the bias, Halston summoned the spirit of these enduring drapes and folds with the knit jersey in the 1970s. The House of Halston continues to pay homage to that aesthetic today.

At every level of the marketplace and from every corner of the globe, the goddess gown continues to spring from the collections of designers who can appreciate its beauty and who wish to interpret it for themselves. Designers can take a cue from this example and explore the degrees of separation that link them and any of their ideas to kindred historical counterparts.

Below: Greek-inspired statue

Right: Floor-length Madeleine Vionnet dress, September 1935

PHOTO: LIPNITZKI/ROGER VIONNET COLLECTION/GETTY IMAGES

Halston fashion show
Autumn/Winter 2008/09
New York City

3 Trends: On, Off, and Adjacent

Although trends are no longer dictated, design houses spend a great deal of time and money trying to predict trends and/or set them into motion. Designers looking to find their place in the market must know whether they intend to be on-trend, trend-adjacent, or off-trend altogether. They must consciously decide whether they will lead, follow, or ignore a trend. Although trend-conscious designers ride the wave of the media and the public's clamoring for examples of the latest fashions, designers who intentionally miss the bandwagon sometimes find that their independent perspectives inadvertently trigger trends or countertrends of their own. On-trend collections will be boiling over with the concept. An alternative approach to the latest craze may be to find smaller and subtler ways to embrace it without making it the focus. The consumer breaks down the same way, and a designer who has a clear understanding of where she stands on trend will connect with the right audience for her product.

Leopard and other animal prints get pulled out of relative obscurity and are presented as fresh and new every few seasons. In fairness, designers will be moved by a trend in different ways from season to season, resulting in new and interesting interpretations of it. If a designer decides to offer the trend du jour as a statement garment, accent piece, and accessory, she makes it easy for clients to adopt at least one interpretation of it on their own terms. Then, of course, there are those who will want to have nothing to do with it. The fashion film classic *Funny Face* depicts the character of fashion editor Maggie Prescott painting the town pink. Someone on her staff asks, "I haven't seen a woman in two weeks in anything but pink. What about you?" Prescott replies, "Me? I wouldn't be caught dead." Truth is, many trends are not merely forecasted, but often made by an industry.

Above: Model Naomi Campbell in leopard print hat, 2004

Below: Anna Wintour in leopard print jacket, 2007

PHOTO BY EVAN AGOSTINI/GETTY IMAGES

PHOTO BY TONY BARSON/WIREIMAGE

Publicity portrait of actress Audrey Hepburn as she wears a wide-brimmed hat and white blouse during the filming of *Funny Face*, directed by Stanley Donen, 1957

4 Corroborating Couture

Fashion history is the next best thing to a time machine for the fashion designer. Contact with authentic artifacts brings the true essence of a time into sharper focus, whether those artifacts are the actual garments and accessories, or illustrations, photos, and film clips. Eras are composed of complexities that involve everything from science to celebrity. The 1950s, for instance, could be a source for fashions informed by the Cold War, teenage culture, foundation garments, rock-and-roll, or popular television programs such as *I Love Lucy*.

Paco Rabanne's fashions in the 1960s were considered "out of this world." At a time when the race to the moon was heating up, visions of a future in space fueled the imaginations of many designers. Rabanne's foray into film led him to team with designer Jacques Fonteray. Together they created the costumes for the cult classic film *Barbarella*. Although many of the clothes in this genre now seem dated, elements of their fashion predictions for the future live on.

Hallmarks of the 1970s include the exploration of androgyny and a growing importance for the relationship between fashion and celebrity. Unisex fashion blurred the lines between the sexes, and even though genderless jumpsuits never became a mainstay, pants played a bigger part in women's fashion than ever before. Fashion became about labels, so much so that they were no longer on the inside of garments but boldly displayed on the back pocket of designer jeans.

Everything was big in the 1980s—hair, jewelry, belts, and most of all, shoulder pads, which were served up in dramatic proportions. Fashion designer and television costumer Nolan Miller is best known for creating the fashions for the cast of the popular 1980s television series *Dynasty*. Careful study of bygone eras (or the current one) can lead designers to consider how they may be able to best define the times they are living in.

Right: Maureen McCormick and Barry Williams rehearse on the set of *The Brady Bunch Hour*, 1977.

Below: Linda Evans, John Forsythe, and Joan Collins, who starred in *Dynasty*

PHOTO BY MICHAEL OCHS ARCHIVES/GETTY IMAGES

PHOTO BY ABC PHOTO ARCHIVES/ABC VIA GETTY IMAGES

Actress Jane Fonda in a publicity still as the title character of Roger Vadim's film *Barbarella*, 1968

5 Forging Identity

"Age cannot wither her ..." These words from Shakespeare best describe Betsey Johnson's staying power in the fashion industry. A Betsey Johnson runway show is not complete until the brand's namesake takes her bow in the form of a cartwheel. Gymnastics aside, the spirit of the gesture is what is important. The brand's the thing in fashion, and in this case, consistency—youthful spirit, flirty femininity, and a wild-child playfulness—is responsible for making Betsey Johnson such a recognizable label.

Great brands have one thing in common: They deliver messages, products, and services that evolve, but never deviate too far from the fundamentals that generated them. Designers can craft an identity with every choice they make.

Designer Betsey Johnson does a signature cartwheel after her spring 2009 collection show at Mercedes-Benz Fashion Week, 2008, in New York City.

PHOTO BY STAN HONDA/AFP/GETTY IMAGES

6 Sensing Style

Each of the five senses plays a significant role in how we interpret fashion, and each should be considered in the design process.

Sight

This is easily the fastest way to assess whether something is pleasing or not. How do shape and scale relate to each other? How vibrant is the color? How dramatic is the contrast?

Touch

This is the second most important factor. How does the material feel against your skin? Does the garment conform to your body and feel comfortable? Is the material soft and pliable, or stiff?

Sound

Imagine the clicks of loose beads knocking into each other; crisp, papery fabrics that rustle as they sway on the body; the synthetic squeak and crunch of plastic as it strains to move.

Smell

Scents have been designed and are chosen to transform environments, camouflage, or seduce. For example, the Thomas Pink label, which primarily sells dress shirts for men and women, pipes a fresh laundered scent into its stores as part of its retail strategy. Although subtle, details such as this serve as a psychological trigger, heightening the fashion experience through aromatherapy.

Taste

Edible garments might seem like the exclusive domain of naughty novelties, but food and fashion have always had a mutually inspirational relationship. Jean Paul Gaultier's dress sculptures made of bread might make the mouth water inasmuch as they could inspire the color, texture, and form of an actual garment. The Salon du Chocolat is a chocolate expo that recognizes the bond between the foodie and the fashionista. A fanciful fashion runway show is a highlight of the event, and features models clad in every kind of cocoa confection.

Fashion designer Jean Paul Gaultier poses with a sculpture of one of his dresses made of bread by French bakers for an exhibition at the Cartier Foundation in Paris, 2004.

PIERRE VERDY/AFP/GETTY IMAGES

Left: Jon Fishman's Sonic Rhythm Dress by Alyce Santoro, Sonic Fabric 2003. Sonic fabric is woven from 50 percent recorded audio cassette tape and 50 percent polyester thread. When gloves equipped with tape heads are rubbed against the fabric the dress makes sound.

Below: Ying Gao's Walking City pneumatic fashions, which are triggered by movement, wind, and touch.

PHOTOS BY DOMINIQUE LAFOND

Human beings have more than just five senses. Consider the sense of balance, acceleration, temperature, kinesthetic, pain, and the sense of direction. Royal Philips Electronics of the Netherlands is working on projects that promise a new level of interaction between apparel and the wearer. Textiles infused with sensors that read and respond to movement, biological variations, and external factors hint at the future of fashion. One example is the SKIN: dress, which uses pattern and color changes to display a person's emotional state.

7 Fashion Equations

The basic arithmetic of dressing can be a useful way to build a collection. Top plus bottom is easy enough, but which top? Which bottom? Once the designer figures out which basics will fit into a collection as well as into a client's wardrobe, he can begin to calculate the variables.

Design details aside, customers have other demands, such as practicality and comfort, when it comes to mixing and matching. The designer must analyze those needs, design components that will fit into the architecture of the collection, and engineer the garments themselves. Broadening a customer's wardrobe of basics or a designer's core line is easy to do. Having more than one variation of each fundamental garment is an effortless way to increase the number of options. Once a structure is in place, it is easy to pull in accessories to keep things interesting.

In 1985, the first Donna Karan collection was launched and it featured her Seven Easy Pieces. The original Easy Pieces were the bodysuit, a wrap skirt, a chiffon blouse, a blazer, a longer jacket, leggings, and a dress; they all remain relevant today. This system of dressing was an important tool for women in the workforce who had a desire to replace their "power suits" with more fashionable choices, and to streamline the decision-making process so that they could put together outfits for the office, travel, or a social occasion at a moment's notice. In 2009, Donna Karan reintroduced her version of the Easy Pieces with an updated list of must-haves: a turtleneck, a skirt, the pant, a jacket, a coat, and jeans.

TECHNICAL DRAWINGS BY MARIE-EVE TREMBLAY

8 Suits of Armor

The instinct to cover our bodies for protection came before the desire to decorate ourselves, initially from the elements and eventually from each other. Combat necessitated the shielding of vulnerable parts of the body during warfare. The major sections of armor broke down into helmet (head), gauntlets (forearms), gorget (neck), breastplate (torso), greaves (legs), and chain mail (for areas that did not allow for rigid plates). It is interesting to note that some of the early versions of bulletproof fabric were made of many layers of silk due to the strength of the fibers. Although Kevlar's ballistic fabric is currently the standard, experiments with spider silk are finding that it has not only comparable strength, but also elasticity.

Modern-day fashion design can provide protection in new, innovative, and relevant ways. In a society that values mobility, the development of lightweight, wearable architecture speaks to fashion designers concerned with social issues such as survival and homelessness. Contemporary visual artist Lucy Orta created the Habitent as part of her exhibition called "Refuge Wear and Body Architecture (1992–1998)." These works examine the common factors that both architecture and fashion design share. They also address a shift in global consciousness regarding what we produce and why.

Right: A model wears a silver ensemble from Jean-Charles de Castelbajac's ready-to-wear show, 2010.

Below: Refuge Wear—Habitent: Aluminum-coated polyamide, two telescopic aluminum poles, whistle, and compass; copyright 2011 by Lucy + Jorge Orta

PHOTO BY JULIEN HEKIMAN/WIREIMAGE

PHOTO: ANNE DE VILLEPOIX GALLERY

A model wears an armor-inspired, silver metal dress by designer Jean-Charles de Castelbajac, 2010.

9 Client Compatibility

Designers, like artists, are often courting their muses for inspiration. They must also cultivate a rich and meaningful relationship with their patrons and those who will partner in promoting their work, such as stylists and celebrities. History provides examples of many successful pairings of artiste and muse. Yves St. Laurent had several prominent sources of creative illumination: former model and fashion icon Betty Catroux, designer Loulou de la Falaise, and actress Cathérine Deneuve, whom he also dressed for films from *Belle de Jour* to *The Hunger*. A lifetime friendship was the basis of the relationship between designer Hubert de Givenchy and actress Audrey Hepburn. Over the years, many lovely women have influenced the House of Chanel, but recently, head designer and creative director Karl Lagerfeld anointed actress Keira Knightley as the Chanel muse. And on the other side of the camera, film director Sofia Coppola is recognized as one of Marc Jacobs' strongest influences.

Having a highly visible individual incorporate your designs into her wardrobe can have a profound effect on a designer. U.S. First Lady Michelle Obama is responsible for shining a light on many talented designers, such as Isabel Toledo and Jason Wu. Toledo has been designing since 1985, but it was the inauguration suit that she designed for Mrs. Obama that put her name on everyone's lips. Later that day, Jason Wu, a relative newcomer, having debuted his first collection in 2006, experienced the same transformation when Michelle Obama wore the now-famous white gown he designed for her to the many inauguration balls.

Whether it is the muse, the benefactor, or the mainstay of every business—the customer—the best relationships are symbiotic ones where both sides learn and benefit from each other.

PHOTO BY DIMITRIOS KAMBOURIS/WIREIMAGE FOR MARC JACOBS

Director Sofia Coppola with designer Marc Jacobs backstage prior to the Marc Jacobs Spring 2009 Fashion Show

U.S. First Lady Michelle Obama stands with inaugural dress designer Jason Wu in front of the gown she wore to the inaugural balls. The gown is now on display at the Smithsonian Museum of American History, Washington, DC.

10 Customization

Even though the desire to fit in is strong, the idea of individuality allows a person to feel special. Faster, more facile manufacturing now allows customers to benefit from lower prices, while still allowing them to enjoy owning something that is truly unique, because they contributed to the design process. Designers of many different types of products are taking advantage of both the tools and consumers' interest in finding this balance between the two.

Compartmentalized design allows the customer to select how the elements of a product are fabricated, creating one-of-a-kind combinations. 9tailors produces quality shirts. Mixing fabrics and choosing specific design details, such as collar, placket, pocket, pocket position, cuff, and cuff button, allows a customer to transform a 9tailors shirt into an original. Converse produces the iconic Chuck Taylor All Star hi-top sneaker, a style that is offered in the traditional canvas, suede, or leather—but that is just the foundation. Customers have many choices when it comes to the design and customization of the shoe, as well as a wide assortment of colors, resulting in infinite design variations.

Based in the Netherlands, fashion designer Berber Soepboer and graphic designer Michiel Schuurman designed the Colour-In Dress, a simple sleeveless dress with an A-line skirt. The third partner in the design process is the wearer. She can use the textile markers provided with the dress to make it her own. The graphic pattern on the textile lends itself to being interpreted in many different ways. The dress also has the potential to be a work in progress, should the wearer decide to add more color each time it is worn.

The whole customization process is particularly successful when the garment itself is familiar and the modifications are easy to imagine. Designers might be wary of giving up complete control, but in all of these examples, the product designers have the unique opportunity to see their design through the eyes of their customers. The exercise provides valuable insight into what their audience wants.

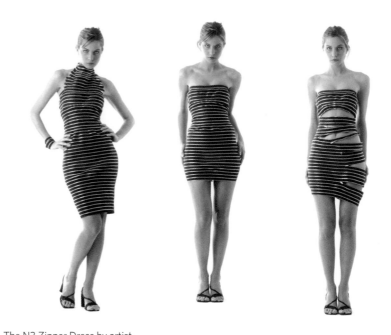

The N3 Zipper Dress by artist designer Sebastian Errazuriz. Made of 120 zippers, this dress allows the wearer to customize neckline, openings, and length simply by zipping or unzipping segments.

Above: Colour-In Dress by Berber Soepboer and Michiel Schuurman, 2008

Right: Customized Converse sneakers

11 Restraint, Impulse, and Impact

Design is as much about what you add to the mix as what you elect not to add. The fabrics, the cut, and the finish must be beyond reproach, because there are no distractions—what you see is what you get. Neutral colors and the absence of adornment are often used to define a restrained aesthetic. Fashion with more of a pop usually relies on something more. This type of design has a pulse, something that can be tapped into, whether it is the vibrant play of color, a stimulating pattern, or the hand of a texture.

Impact can have many of the qualities of impulse, but it is not restrained to passion or theatricality. Sometimes this type of forceful fashion can be downright hideous. The role of ugly fashion is to challenge. Observers can't help but be engaged, whether they find themselves intrigued or offended. The love-hate relationship teeters on design sensibilities. Will purposefully dowdy, discordant, or garish creations be interesting? Or does a runway oddity disturb and unsettle you? The point is that regardless of whether you like something you don't understand you cannot dismiss it, because it has grabbed your attention. It can be appreciated merely for having been able to shake things up and penetrate established standards of beauty far enough to challenge you.

A model wearing a Hussein Chalayan creation, 2010

12 Mind Mapping

A truly creative mind is one that builds a foundation with the left brain so that the right brain can make giant leaps of fancy. It's easy to identify and focus on what our brain has a natural tendency to be good at, and to disregard weakness. Strengthening those shortcomings is a key to success. Lefties are analytical, technical, critical, and logical. They need to stretch to tap into the part of their brain that allows them to be more intuitive, imaginative, and innovative. The same level of effort should be put into planning, organizing, and building structure for a right-brain individual.

Simultaneously entertaining opposing needs and desires can be a tough thing to contain in your brain. In order to overcome natural tendencies that lean to one side or the other, a designer needs to move the process outside of her head. There are several ways to map out a successful creative strategy that allows the designer to see, sort, and shuffle everything involved.

Left-brain fashion thinking can be found in a designer's ability to analyze the needs of the market; make reasonably logical decisions; craft language that will best represent their vision; have an awareness and basic comprehension of innovations in science and technology; and be well-versed in the value of numbers in patternmaking as well as in business.

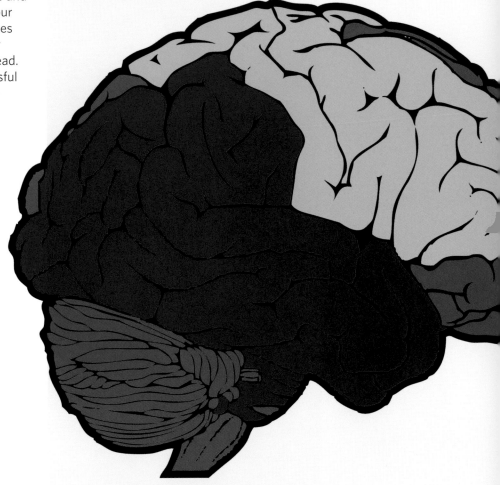

Right-brain fashion thinking can be found in a designer's ability to consider the process of design thoughtfully; trust their intuition when making decisions; always be open to creative insights and exercises; appreciate the art of fashion; and find the music that creates an appropriate setting for their work.

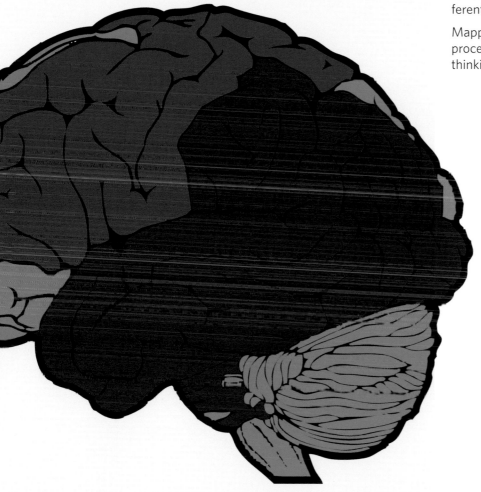

Talk it out. Every designer can use a sounding board. Hearing ideas out loud is a great reality check, made even better when others provide you with feedback.

Write it out. Committing it to paper allows one thought to lead to another on the page, without the risk of letting any idea slip through your fingers.

Lay it out. The wide open space of a table, a bulletin board, or a wall allows the designer to spread out all aspects of an idea. When a designer can see the whole picture she will begin to recognize relationships between the many different elements.

Mapping things out is a way to fine-tune the process and enhance the potential for original thinking.

13 Net and Narrow

The world of haute couture is so elite and exclusive that many designers feel they need to allude to it in their work, if not aspire to it. Although it has a very narrow audience, couture has a compelling allure because that audience is composed of some of the richest, most famous, and most powerful fashion clients in the world. This niche crowd certainly has its perks, if only by association. Serving this aristocratic caste of couture well will often come with critical acclaim, but not always economic success. Fashion designers who support their visionary projects with more mainstream creations are the ones who have staying power.

Ready-to-wear reaches the people en masse. The only limitations when serving vast numbers are manufacturing outlets and developing products that have mass appeal. Casting such a wide net not only generates greater sales, but also builds name recognition. Just because it is off the rack doesn't mean it cannot have great influence. In 1994, rapper Snoop Dogg wore a Tommy Hilfiger shirt on an episode of *Saturday Night Live*. The black, urban, rap subculture responded almost immediately. Hilfiger's work was adopted and adapted by hip-hop followers everywhere. Hilfiger cultivated relationships with other leaders in this community and a retail star was born. This was enough to place Hilfiger on the map, but he realized he needed to serve this audience by scaling the clothes up in size, styling his work to reflect the culture, and turning his logo into a highly visible status symbol in the fashion community. His large customer base continues to inform the direction of his work. The rest is fashion business history.

Musician/actor LL Cool J and designer Tommy Hilfiger, 2007

14 Disposable as Investment

Nontextile projects are commonly used to stretch a fashion designer's creative muscles. Many fashion programs offer at least one course that requires a student designer to build a body covering without fabric and conventional sewing methods. The exploration of this type of wearable art involves a great deal of experimentation. What are the objects of choice? How will they be assembled or woven into a surface? How will components such as the bodice, skirt, and sleeve be put together? What kind of method of closure will be devised? The final product takes shape as a form sculpted to fit the body and mimic traditional apparel.

Depending on the nature of the raw materials in a garment of this category, it might not have a long life span—a tissue-paper gown's days are numbered. So, why invest in such a disposable piece of fashion? The novelty and artistic value of garments made out of paper bags, plastic spoons, or duct tape are inherent, but there is a greater value to be found. The results of bringing fashion design sensibilities to nontraditional projects include unexpected problem-solving methods and inspired techniques. Compositions, color schemes, textures, and construction solutions that might not have otherwise been used to create conventional clothing become apparent. A new set of skills and a fresh perspective can kick-start a collection.

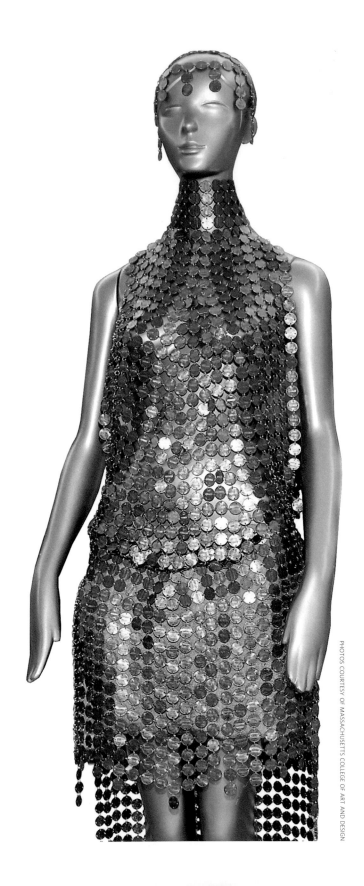

PHOTOS COURTESY OF MASSACHUSETTS COLLEGE OF ART AND DESIGN

Left: Nontextile dress constructed out of pennies by Ines Antigua

Right: Nontextile dress constructed out of teabags by Kathryn Feeley

15 Environmental Context

Geographical regions develop a style of their own. In the United States alone, the North and the South have distinctly divergent tastes for clothing. The West Coast and the East Coast have very different takes on the definition of fashion. The Midwest has another standard of style altogether. Instead of making value judgments about the worthiness of a certain sensibility, a good designer will delve into the roots these assessments stem from. These foundations are usually based on the many aspects of an environment that would color our choices: historical events, cultural influences, geography, and climate. When this concept is extended globally there are even subtler differences to be studied.

A good fashion compass will help uncover the reasons for understanding why a wardrobe of black has become synonymous with urban settings such as New York. Is the inclination to adopt such a dark palette just a practical choice? Is the overall look harder and more intimidating, something that might give you an edge when dealing with the gritty realities of the city?

What is the explanation for an inclination toward bright colors and bold patterns in the South? Does the weather play a part in it? Do these choices reflect the landscape? This examination assists designers in delivering their product to a market that is already prone to receive it well.

COURTESY OF POOR LITTLE RICH GIRL, BOSTON

Left: Vintage Yves Saint Laurent dress in bright, colorful floral print

Right: Sophisticated, dark brown cascade collar suit by Sara Campbell

16 Acquisitions

Setting up a business or starting a project requires that designers shift into hunter-gatherer mode. What are the means by which they will be able to develop work? How will they amass resources?

Good fashion hunters will familiarize themselves with a terrain, track their target, and acquire it. Identifying the right machinery and the proper tools is essential. Not all cutting instruments are created equal. For instance, the difference between scissors and shears is length; the latter must measure more than 6 inches (15 cm). Design rooms will reserve shears for cutting fabrics versus scissors for cutting paper. Pinking shears, appliqué scissors, and snips each make specific jobs a little easier.

Fashion gatherers are a little more subjective. They will forage through the many choices of fabrics and notions to procure the ideal raw materials, based on aesthetic needs and seasonal demands.

Once a workroom is outfitted and its shelves are stocked with supplies, a workforce must be assembled. In doing so, the designer must determine how each member of the staff fits into the community being crafted. Next, the designer must build a culture, an environment, systems, and technology.

In some cases, it is a smart idea to accumulate reserves. A surplus can mean the difference between enduring and throwing in the towel when faced with situations that challenge survival. However, stockpiling isn't helpful unless the goods are relevant and are actually put to use. The value of a designer's inventory—comprising machinery, raw materials, manpower, or finished product—depends on how cohesive it all is.

Right: Design studio: button bins

Far Right: Design studio: fabric and pattern storage

PHOTO: JOEL BENJAMIN

PHOTO: JOEL BENJAMIN

17 Collaboration

Some very successful fashion design teams prove that two heads are often better than one. A creative collaboration can result in designs that are more complex and innovative than those that originate from a singular vision. Partnerships with buyers, editors, clients, and other designers all have the potential to foster successful ideas and enhance the creative process.

Some examples of successful fashion design teams include:

- **Viktor Horsting** and **Rolf Snoeren** of Viktor & Rolf met while studying fashion at the Arnhem Academy of Art and Design in The Netherlands. Their team approach to fashion continues to surprise and charm the fashion elite.

- Parsons School of Design in New York City was where **Lazaro Hernandez** and **Jack McCollough** both studied before going on to form the label Proenza Schouler—a name that keeps it all in the family, originating from the maiden names of both designers' mothers.

- **Domenico Dolce** met **Stefano Gabbana** while working for the same design firm in Milan, Italy, and are now the force behind Italian luxury house Dolce and Gabbana, a multimillion-dollar fashion empire.

- Sibling camaraderie, not rivalry, is at the heart of the sister team of **Kate** and **Laura Mulleavy** for Rodarte, a company also named after their mother's maiden name. They have collaborated with the Gap as well as Target, proving they understand how to interface well with others.

- Power couple **Isabel** and **Ruben Toledo** represent the husband and wife duo that impact culture on multiple fronts. She is a fashion designer and he is an artist.

Above: Ruben and Isabel Toledo

Right: Dutch designers Rolf Snoeren (left) and Viktor Horsting (right), of Viktor & Rolf, shake hands at the end of their Autumn/Winter 2010/11 ready-to-wear collection show in Paris.

18 Articulation of Style

Use your words. A designer benefits greatly from a mastery of language—not merely having an extensive vocabulary, but also possessing the ability to craft words into ideas, messages, and stories. Whether complex or uncomplicated, the intent behind the words that are used to describe and define things helps to inspire and develop design concepts. Through language, a designer can discover a direction for a project.

Using color as an example, the adjectives used to narrow the definition of a color can affect the context in which the final product is perceived. Just red? It should never be just red. Perhaps it is ruby, a red as rich and luxurious as the gemstone. Or cherry red, a color you can almost taste. When you think of Ferrari the associations are sport, speed, and Italy, which makes Ferrari's co-branding of sneakers and athletic sportswear a natural fit.

Although designers may work from a broad palette, they can also become closely associated with a particular color. Elsa Schiaparelli is forever linked with shocking pink, just as Valentino will always be remembered for his signature red.

It may just seem like semantics, but the same is true of all the vital components involved in developing a garment or a central theme for a collection. A smooth texture can be described as having a glossy, polished, or satin finish, whereas a grainy texture can be described as rough, porous, or earthy. Clever wordplay is at the heart of how fashion is discussed in the media, so why not start that dialogue in-house on the designer's terms.

Models in red, Valentino's signature color, walk on the catwalk for a grand finale, 2008.

PHOTO BY DOMINIQUE CHARRIAU/WIREIMAGE

19 Building and Breaking Templates

Establishing standards provides a fashion designer with reference points. Finding the middle is important. The "average" should not be considered a death sentence to creativity, when it is positioned as the starting point. Once specifications are in place, understood, and respected, a designer can bend, if not break, all the rules.

The basic sloper is employed as a foundation for flat patternmaking because it contains all the vital measurements to build a pattern that will correspond to the body it is being designed for. With those measurements in place, almost any modification is possible, while still keeping the function and fit of the garment grounded in reality. A fitting muslin is a garment that can be used in much the same way. This garment is constructed so that a designer can manipulate the design and customize the fit.

Good croquis figures are based on the proportions of the human body. When the relationships between parts of the body are maintained, the figure can be exaggerated to extremes without risking abstraction. The transformation may reflect the designer's style tendencies, but the finished product will remain recognizable.

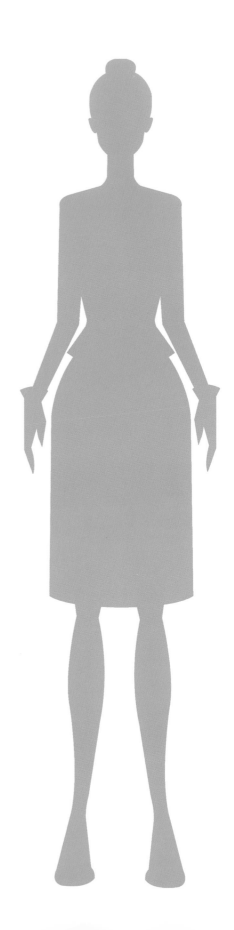

Left: Average length and elongated croquis

Right: Various croquis exaggerations designed to accentuate overall silhouette

20 Pattern Instruments

A sharp pencil, some paper, and a ruler—it seems simple enough, but patternmaking demands that designers filter their vision of a garment through a strict mathematical grid. There is no getting away from the fact that well-executed patterns rely heavily on geometry and are the result of thinking like an engineer. Designers should be very familiar with the purpose of each tool of the trade and fluent in the language of whatever units of measurement they are working in, down to the smallest fraction.

Precise measurements and clear notations are key when making pieces fit together. Notches, for instance, provide the stitcher with specific places where pieces are to be joined. They serve as anchor points, which help to ensure proper assembly. Seam allowance can be looked at as the breakdown lane of stitching lines, because they give us room to handle the fabric while we are sewing and provide room for alterations after the fact—too much and you have unwanted bulk; too little and seams begin to fall apart. Beyond taking each flat piece and attaching it to another, these two-dimensional pieces may also be manipulated into more nuanced three-dimensional shapes. Tailoring a garment to the human form might require darts that eliminate unwanted fullness, or gathers that add it where desired.

A commercial pattern comes with a set of instructions that take the consumer through the most efficient way of putting a garment together. Part of the design process for the designer should include creating a similar algorithm for a pattern addressing which methods of construction will be used, and what the specific sequence of steps will be.

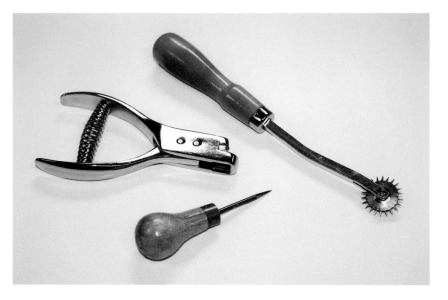

Above: Tracing wheel, notcher, and awl

Right: Pattern rack

21 Stitching Tools

Sewing is a sensory experience. Following instructions that are provided in a book, a video, or a live demonstration is a start, but there is no substitute for experience, and lots of it, when it comes to stitching a garment together. Easing the cap of a sleeve into an armhole is definitely easier said than done. Only repetition will provide the experience needed to handle the fabric expertly, select the proper thread, and understand how to control and maximize the tools you are working with. Nothing is perfect, but practice certainly gets you close.

There are many choices when it comes to what type of stitch to use for any given job, and each can be executed by hand or on a machine:

- Loose single-thread stitches for basting

- Blanket or overlock stitches to finish an edge

- Pad stitching to secure layers of fabric together

- Back stitches or tacking to reinforce areas

- Zigzag or top stitching to decorate the surface

- Chain, cross, or satin stitches for embroidery

- Buttonhole stitches to finish and reinforce the opening for a button closure

- Blind stitches for hemming

In every case, a light, seemingly effortless touch is the mark of the professional.

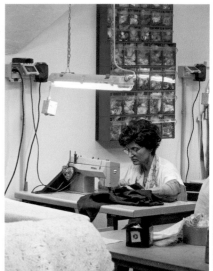

PHOTOS: JOEL BENJAMIN

Above Left: Hand sewing

Above Right: Machine sewing

Right: Basting samples

Far Right: Hand basting

PHOTO: JOEL BENJAMIN

22 Rendering Media

Fashion renderings are usually created in pencil, marker, or paint. Today, the pixel is another medium for drawing fashion with the aid of computer software. Whether it's a fashion note on a napkin, style schematics in a notebook, or fashion shorthand in chalk on a chalkboard, the goal is the exchange of ideas.

There is a mystique around the art of fashion, as though only a select few are entitled to even attempt to create it. Although not everyone who sits down to draw will produce art to rival the work of Steven Stipelman or Antonio Lopez, it's important to remember that these masters are illustrators and not designers. Honing the skills required to commit concepts to paper is primarily about hand to eye coordination, which only comes with time and practice.

A carefully conceived drawing, in which style lines, design details, and proportions have been thoughtfully planned out, will help make the next step—draping and/or patternmaking—move that much faster.

Right: French designer Yves Saint Laurent using chalk to sketch fashion designs on a chalkboard in the atelier of the House of Christian Dior, where he has just been named as successor to couturier Christian Dior, Paris, November 1957.

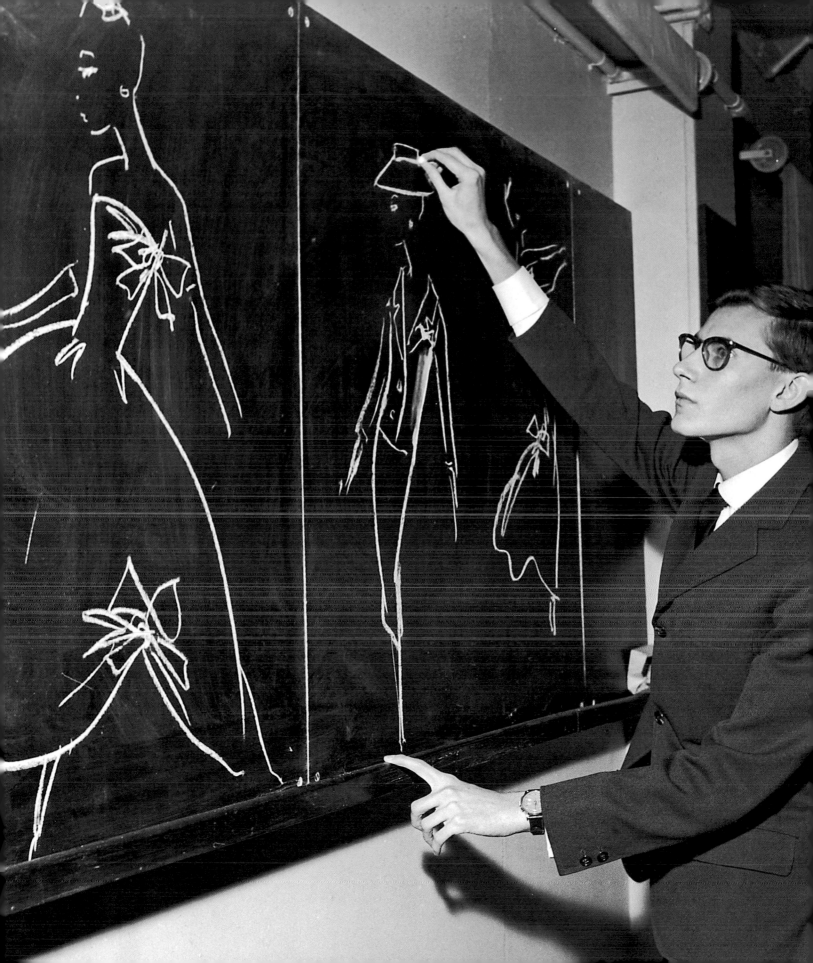

23 Taming Textiles

Textiles are a very tangible source of inspiration. Much like the marble that informs the sculptor what it wants to become, fabric will suggest what shapes and types of manipulation will transform it into a work of art.

The same pattern for a garment will assume uniquely different characteristics, depending on whether it is made of silk chiffon, ribbed knit, ripstop nylon, Lycra, taffeta, or wool felt. The designer can design with fabrics based on how they coordinate and contrast with each other. Weight, body, and weave will provide further direction. Color, pattern, and texture also deliver a whole set of additional choices.

A designer can take ideas for a collection into new territory by switching fabrics. Substituting fabrics like denim for taffeta, chiffon for oxford cloth, leather for linen, and lace for tweed is one way to trigger unpredictable innovations. Blocking with color, pattern, and texture is another way to shake things up. Combine these methods with techniques usually reserved for different fabrics, and the design choices multiply. Apply a top-stitched flat-felled seam, commonly found on denim, to silk organdy and it brings together two seemingly unrelated areas of fashion, creating something fresh and unexpected.

PHOTO: JOEL BENJAMIN

Right: Medium body: Sara Campbell floral jacquard skirt

Below: Full body: Viktor & Rolf silver dipped satin skirt

Light body: soft satin
charmeuse blouse

24 Letters: Slopers

A sloper is a template for any pattern piece that does not include seam allowance. Starting from scratch is not always necessary. It is used to develop variations on patterns and is a great tool for brainstorming and testing out design ideas without having to go back to square one. Since a good sloper already includes all the measurements that will ensure a proper fit, the designer has the freedom to concentrate on aesthetics. The designer can manipulate the position of a dart, add fullness, lengthen or shorten, as well as cut away or build areas onto the original.

Each sloper piece is like a letter in the DNA of a garment. Each of these base patterns is designed to conform to a different part of the body as well as interfacing with other pieces. Every template has elements that are unique to that piece. In a sleeve, the seam that closes it does not relate to any part of another pattern piece. But the cap of the sleeve must fit into an armhole that is created when the front bodice is connected to the back bodice at the shoulder and side seams. The most essential aspect of designing something that goes from two dimensions to three is fit— how the pieces fit together and how they fit the purpose.

Getting wrapped up in the minutia of this blueprint for a garment may seem like the exclusive domain of patternmakers, but designers can use their own sensibilities to solve design challenges with this as well.

Slopers

25 Words: Garments

Every garment makes a valuable contribution to an overall look. It might be cast in the starring role or as a supporting piece. Individual items of clothing can be treated like the words that will be expressing the designer's vision. Big words as well as little ones should be carefully chosen, because even the slightest variation in definitions can make a big difference.

The original stimulus for a designer's inspiration can be distilled into subtle but powerful details in even the simplest of garments. In addition to being appreciated by the true connoisseur, these touches add a complexity that makes these garments distinct. Although some items are intended to emphasize a more dominant piece, they should never be treated like an afterthought. If they are designed as independent entities, they will stand alone in terms of design and quality.

A simple white blouse by Viktor & Rolf, made distinctive with button detail, 2006

26 Sentences: Ensembles

Assembling an ensemble is like stringing words together to form a sentence. In the best of situations, the resultant fashion phrase is a well-calibrated combination of references that inspired the design process in the first place.

Mixing drastically different colors can punch up a look. Blending more harmonious shades will result in a gentler touch. At either end of the spectrum or anywhere in between, color should always allude to the impact the designer wishes to have on his audience.

The interplay of textures and patterns can also be used to stimulate or relax the person wearing those specific garments. Finding the right balance between different shapes is an important factor, whether the designer wants the complete look to have a reserved silhouette or one with dramatic flair. Ornament can be scaled to different proportions so that it has the desired effect. The lack of it can be just as bold in its austerity.

Designers need to consider that these sets of garments will not exist in a vacuum, and they need to make their mark on the observer—the client's circle, the media, and the general public. Every designer has the ability to make clear statements of style with every composition.

PHOTO: JESSICA WEISER

Samira Vargas ensembles featuring a mix of texture and pattern, 2010

PHOTO: JESSICA WEISER

27 Stories: Collections

A variety of looks can be brought together to illustrate a bigger idea. The mix itself is an extension of the concept that inspired each element of the collection to begin with. Many choices are involved in designing a single garment, creating corresponding pieces to put together an outfit, and then doing that numerous times until you have all the ingredients necessary to tell your fashion story: a collection.

The designer must think like a stylist and consider how these pieces will go together to craft a bigger, more complex picture. Ask the questions that would help you craft a good story. Have you a made conscious choice to juxtapose contrasting elements to create conflict and drama? Is humor woven into the collection that connects with your audience through witty choices? Is there a sense of harmony in how your choices come together? Does each ensemble feel like it represents a character in your story? Do you have a strong start and an exciting finish?

The specific decisions a designer makes—putting emphasis on what she sees as important—will ultimately set her apart from other designers and their collections. This process is just as important as the garments themselves, because it places the designer's vision in a context of her own creation.

Christian Lacroix Collection, 2006

28 Punctuation: Details

Once the structure of a garment has been clearly defined and the materials being used to fabricate it have been chosen, it is time to contemplate the details. These points will fine-tune the design and ensure that a designer's aesthetic sensibilities are consistent throughout. Well-placed embellishments will punctuate the design, but not distract from it.

Decorative buttons or snaps help to mix form and function. One big, bold button on an otherwise understated coat serves as an exclamation point. Most fans of the classic Western-style shirt would agree that pearl snaps are an essential finishing touch. Big brassy zippers stress utility, and when used deliberately they can make a statement. Exposing that kind of heavy hardware and having it slash through a delicate dress definitely makes a declaration.

Strictly ornamental details such as embroidery or beading are straightforward enough, except when they are strategically placed in unexpected locations. A small godet inserted at the end of a seam can provide ease but also interest. Topstitching with thread in an accent color is one way to underline the style lines of a garment. The edge of a garment may be dotted and dashed with a decorative blanket stitch.

For many fashion designers, "the devil is in the details" because that is where they might find the process the most difficult or challenging. It is also a way that designers can subtly sign their masterpieces.

Above: Beaded Mary McFadden gown

Right: Decorative zipper detail by Aey Hotarwaisaya

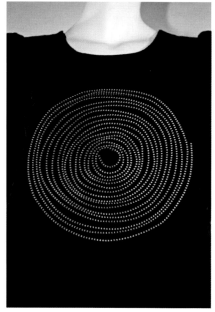

Beaded, bowed, and gilded
dress by Christian Lacroix,
2006

29 Closures

Closure methods are primarily practical considerations, but they can also be used as prominent design details that complete a look. Almost any fastener can be stealthily hidden within a placket or a seam, or camouflaged when covered in fabric, to achieve a clean appearance. There are also special considerations for each type of closure that will affect the fit and finish of a garment.

Flat buttons are common in most instances, but shanked buttons are often used when the thickness of the fabric requires greater space to allow for that bulk to be buttoned. A standard zipper can be centered, lapped, or inserted without any extensions of fabric to intentionally remain visible. The invisible zipper is designed to pull the fabric on both sides together to mimic a seam.

Hooks and eyes as well as snaps are available in different sizes, colors, and types. In some instances, they are covered to blend into the garment. Both also are available on a tape that can be sewn in. Velcro is commonly not visible and can be applied in segments or continuous strips. Elements such as ties, belts, frogs, and toggles are usually chosen for their decorative contribution as well as their usefulness.

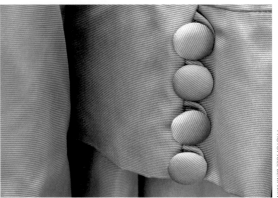

PHOTO: JOEL BENJAMIN

Top: Pink bias ribbon lacing

Above: Blue fabric-covered buttons

30 Specialty Requisites

Special materials are often required to achieve desired effects, provide specific functionality, and ensure quality workmanship. Solving unique design challenges requires different materials. If the right ingredients don't exist, an innovative designer will be inspired to invent them.

A full-flowing skirt will benefit from a band of horsehair braid sewn into the hem. Originally made of actual horsehair, this mesh is now made of nylon. One of its uses includes providing a flexible stiffness that reinforces the edge of the hem. The skirt might be made without it, but including it results in a rounded, billowing hemline that seems to roll as it moves.

In weatherproof outerwear, a lack of breathability might require the insertion of a nylon mesh into strategically placed vents. Double zippers allow the garment to be partially opened at either end without completely exposing the wearer to the elements.

Thread is at the heart of putting together most garments. Each project will require a different type of thread. The size and weight of a thread is indicated by a set of numbers, such as 50/3. The first number refers to the diameter of each strand (the higher the number the finer the thread) and the second to the number of strands that have been twisted together to create that thread. Finer threads are in keeping with hand-work and delicate fabrics. Strong threads will hold up to heavier fabrics and can be used in situations when there will be additional stress, as in gathering stitches and buttonholes. Synthetic threads provide a little more give when sewing knits. Embroidery thread is more commonly referred to as floss and is usually composed of six loosely twisted strands.

In addition to different lengths and diameters, the shape of the point of a needle is very important. For instance, needles used for knits need to be slightly rounded at the point so they don't snag.

Clockwise: Decorative yarns; heavy-duty zipper; thread; horsehair

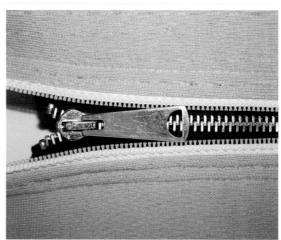

31 Miscellaneous Markers

In fashion, everything revolves around the new and the unexplored. Like anything else, even the fashion industry can fall into a rut, and only random wild cards are able to shake things up and shift the fashion landscape just enough to influence change. In truth, they deserve their own custom, sometimes complex, label, but because it is difficult to fit them into a category, these fashion flares are usually filed under "Miscellaneous." Their randomness should not belie their importance in terms of inspiration and direction.

Now that virtually everyone has a blog of his own, the blogosphere's impact seems diluted and commonplace. However, the blogging landscape is still a place where diamonds in the rough can be found. These undiscovered gems reflect facets of fashion that may not have been on anyone's radar until one of these writers chooses to focus on it and spread the word. Some are described as being on the front lines of fashion, so tapping into the right combination of online voices will provide insight, resources, and inspiration for the fashion designer.

Blogs are just one example. Movements toward sustainability and fair trade have been building momentum in the fashion industry, but they rarely gain traction in the high-end fashion world. However, in the June 2009 issue of *Vogue*, Cameron Diaz was featured wearing a pair of eco-friendly/high-end fashion shorts by Goods of Conscience, a fashion label created by Father Andrew O'Connor, a Catholic priest based in the Bronx, New York. The unexpected source certainly generates interest, but the business model and the message lay the groundwork for the evolution of an industry.

Designers need to be looking for signs of the future on all fronts—who is shining a light on a different perspective and how that will fuel their creative process.

Father Andrew O'Connor, (right), created Goods of Conscience in answer to the needs of several communities. The company employs both Mayan Indian weavers and underemployed Bronx sewers, supporting local production in both locales. The line uses a soft, lightweight material made of organic cotton, called Social Fabric, which is made in the Guatemalan tradition of back-strap weaving. The manufacturing of the fabric and garments takes into account important issues of sustainability and fair trade that face the fashion industry as well as the consumer.

PHOTO: COURTESY OF GOODS OF CONSCIENCE

Tavi Gevinson is an American fashion blogging phenomenon. She started "Style Rookie" in 2008 at the age of eleven and her followers include Miuccia Prada, John Galliano, Rei Kawakubo, and the Mulleavy sisters. These design stars say she "gets it," and they are taking notice.

32 Care and Feeding of a Garment

It's imperative to consider the life of a garment when designing it, such as how the garment will hold up over time, through wear, cleaning, and steaming. This can make the difference between having an object that is a keepsake and one that is relegated to the dustbin. In some cases, it is the patina that develops during the aging process that adds to its desirability. In others, the value comes from the item's ability to retain a good-as-new appearance over time.

Will the garment's fabric and construction stand up to machine washing, or will it require hand washing or dry cleaning? Will a lint brush or an adhesive roller be able to clear the surface of lint, hair, and fuzz?

Does the fabric require pressing or steaming? In the case of velvet or corduroy fabrics, will a needle press board or pad help maintain the pile? When ironing the garment, how will a tailor's ham, a press mitt, a seam roll, a point press, or a sleeve board work for the user? Will a press cloth or pad help to prevent the fabric from shining or singeing?

After a length of time, folds can become permanent and weaken the fabric, so proper storage is essential. Which type of hanger best suits that particular garment? Will packing with tissue and cardboard forms help keep the body of the garment in shape and wrinkle-free? Would it be best to store the garment on the hanger in a plastic bag or a cloth bag, or in a box with acid-free paper? Will basting pockets and vents closed help prevent sagging or twisting?

Designers may not always have the time to test the endurance of a garment, but they can become familiar with how fabrics and construction techniques will stand up to time and use, helping them to make the best choices.

Faux furs can be brushed gently to prevent matting, also removing dust and debris. May be machine washed and hung to dry. No dryer or direct heat.

Nylon, polyester, and other synthetics used for outerwear may be machine washed or dry cleaned. They can also be placed in a dryer at a low temperature.

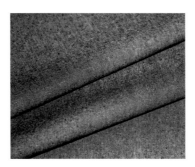

Sturdy cotton (canvas, denim twill) can be laundered—hot water for whites; warm or cold for colors. Shrinkage can be addressed with prewashing.

Dry cleaning is preferred for most delicate silks. They may also be gently hand washed with mild soap. Lay flat to dry on a noncolored towel.

Heavy wool tweeds and suiting may be dry cleaned or spot cleaned with a damp sponge. A steamer is the recommended way to take out wrinkles.

Hairy fabrics (angora, mohair, alpaca, or vicuna) should be dry cleaned or gently washed. Do not wring or agitate; dry flat. Steam; do not iron flat.

Raw silks and linens can be dry cleaned or gently hand washed. They may be pressed at a low heat from the reverse side of the fabric or steamed.

Fabrics with metallic or plastic threads should be dry cleaned. A press cloth should be used when ironing on low temperature from the reverse side.

Pile fabrics (velvet, terry cloth, or corduroy) can be cleaned according to fiber content. Steam only from the reverse side or on a needle press board.

Right: For the designer working with exotic trims such as fur or feathers, it is a good idea to design the garment so that these sections are removable for cleaning purposes. Gown by designer Nara Paz

33 Ancient Tools and Techniques

For the first time on record, the woman who has been charged with creating braid work used to decorate Chanel suits since 1947 was introduced to the public in the documentary *Signé Chanel*. Madame Pouzieux creates the famous fashion braids on a one-of-a-kind ancient loom. Working the loom is second nature to her, but many apprentices have been confounded by its intricacies. The House of Chanel is a loyal patron of her work, because this type of braid trim can be found nowhere else.

This story illustrates one example of how valuable and unique old-world techniques can be, not to mention antique tools and machinery. New sewing machines with built-in computers can be programmed to do many wonderful things, but for power and stability, nothing compares to older industrial machines. While the machines can still be found, the knowledge and skill required to maintain them is becoming hard to find. Many talents are also fading into obscurity, because these vintage crafts are not being passed on. Although automation affords the designer the ability to produce faster, the process of researching, learning, and implementing old-fashioned methods may prove to be a useful creative exercise.

Left Above: Vintage sewing machine

Left Below: Loom

Right: Assorted braids by f8

34 Accessory Closet

Which comes first, the suit or the stilettos? What about the current "it" bag or a smart pair of glasses? A great accessory can be the centerpiece of a great outfit. If the shopper can take that approach, why can't the designer? Great accessories that straddle the line between function and art are worthy of a designer's attention. Studying the microcosms of style may generate ideas that a designer can expand upon, and possibly build a collection around.

Hats are not a must for today's fashionable woman the way they were in the 1950s and 1960s, but they have not gone away. Milliners are regularly required to rise to the challenge of empowering their customers with the confidence to don these artful expressions of fashion. Apparel designers can take a cue from the craft and artistry behind their work.

Shoes have become one of the most important fashion accessories, because unless the option of going barefoot is on the table, a pair of shoes is technically a necessity. According to Answers.com, on average, women between the ages of twenty-five and fifty own from forty to sixty pairs of shoes. As a fashion category, shoes rule!

PHOTO: JOEL BENJAMIN

Clockwise: Fashionable eyewear; Shaunt Sarian bag; Zack Lo shoes

PHOTO: TRACY AIGUIER

PHOTO: SIMPLYNATE PHOTOGRAPHY

Marie Galvin hat

35 Vintage Patina

Younger siblings everywhere complain about hand-me-downs, but in fashion, a secondhand garment has the potential to be a truly coveted item. Its degree of value stems from many things:

- Is the garment still relevant? A great motorcycle jacket sends just as powerful a message as it ever did.

- Does a designer label count? Identifiable markers speak to the power of branding fashion.

- Is it a symbolic part of history? The ultra-feminine silhouettes of the early 1960s have greatly influenced contemporary fashion thanks to the popularity of the television series *Mad Men*.

- How rare is the item? One-of-a-kind pieces are sought after regardless of the category.

- Who wore it? The provocative dress that Marilyn Monroe wore to sing "Happy Birthday" to President John F. Kennedy in 1962 was noteworthy in its day, but has continued to increase exponentially in both popularity and value since then.

- Does it possess glamour by association? Designers and journalists are often guilty of fostering relationships between clothing and celebrities, even if there is no credible affiliation between the two. Describing a little black dress as "very Audrey Hepburn" may be a sort of tribute to her, Givenchy, and *Breakfast at Tiffany's*, but there isn't a real connection.

In what way can today's designers brush the patina of a vintage garment over their work? It need not be as literal as tarnished buttons and buckles or distressed and faded fabrics. The subtle use of color schemes that reflect the aesthetics of another time is an option. The application of old-world patternmaking, construction, or finishing techniques is another. The use of silhouettes that reference specific periods in fashion history can also provide the designer with a sense of another era. Vintage sources are now varied and plentiful. Local boutiques, regional markets, and online retailers are useful barometers that allow a designer to spot timely vintage trends.

Right: "IT'S MINE!" A *Daily News* front-page headline from October 28, 1999. Collector Bob Schagrin pays $1.1 million for Marilyn Monroe's dress.

PHOTO: NY DAILY NEWS ARCHIVE/GETTY IMAGES

Evening gown featuring a distinctive geometric silhouette of the 1980s

COURTESY OF POOR LITTLE RICH GIRL, BOSTON

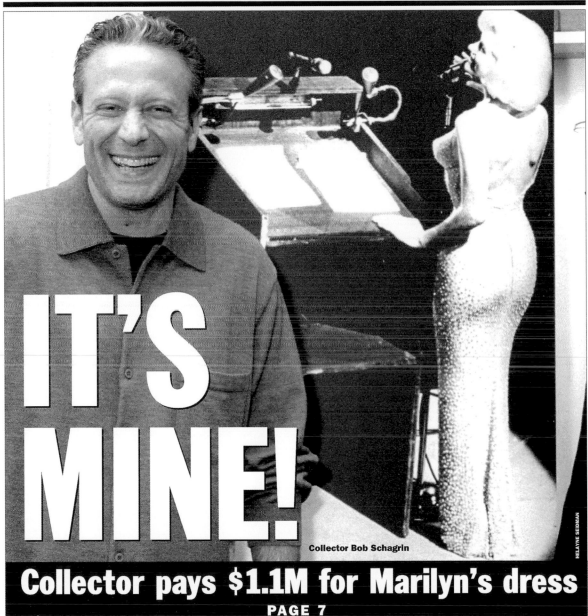

NEWS · BUSINESS · FEATURES · SPORTS

GORE GOES ON OFFENSIVE IN DEBATE
PAGES 4 & 5

17 MILLION HOT DOGS RECALLED
PAGE 2

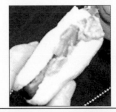

LAPTOPS GO HOME WITH SCHOOL KIDS
SPECIAL REPORT
PAGES 32 & 33

DAILY ◉ NEWS

NEW YORK'S HOMETOWN NEWSPAPER

Thursday, October 28, 1999

IT'S MINE!

Collector Bob Schagrin

HELAYNE SEIDMAN

Collector pays $1.1M for Marilyn's dress

PAGE 7

77

36 Fashion Translations

Fashion influences come from many different sources, including sports, clubs, social and economic class, and different cultures. It's up to the designer to translate and adopt these influences to fit into the mainstream.

The rugby shirt, for example, allows teams to identify themselves with team-specific colors incorporated into the five or six horizontal stripes called *hoops*. The "rep" tie is used by schools, clubs, and military regiments to display their affiliations. The term *rep* refers to the ribbing of the fabric's weave, not the color and configuration of stripes (a common misconception). How might the idea of wearing your "colors" figure in the design process?

Interesting distinctions develop among different social and economic classes. In the United Kingdom, costermongers, who sold fruit and vegetables from market stalls, would set themselves apart from other vendors by sewing a row of pearl buttons along the seams of their garments. The result was called a Flash Boy outfit. A large cargo of pearl buttons from Japan in the 1860s is said to have contributed to the development of this trend among the tradesmen.

Henry Croft was a part of that community, and he is credited with creating the unique Pearly Kings and Queens look in 1875. Croft, a teenage orphan who had a desire to help those in need, understood that he needed to set himself apart to be noticed, so he covered an entire suit with pearl buttons. The first "pearly" was born. The working class adopted the Pearly Kings and Queens tradition to continue the "whip around," which is what they called making collections for those in need.

Denim garments have been interpreted and reinterpreted over the years. Introduced as work clothes and then adopted as fashion by teenagers, denim went on to serve as a canvas for such embellishments as metal studs, hand painting, and rhinestones. Sometimes the fusion of two different fashion languages can result in a fresh new idea—denim and pearly buttons.

Mary and Fred Tinsley, Pearly Queen and King of Southwark, London, 1949

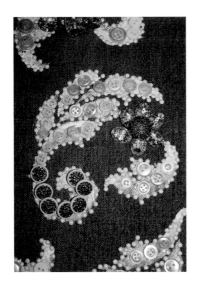

Decorative button detail on
denim from Art by T

37 Four Seasons: A Timeline

The seasons help compartmentalize fashion. The practical demands of weather alone cause us to focus on the elements of design that shield a person from the rain, sun, wind, or snow. However, the natural aesthetics of each period also influence designers with regard to the colors, patterns, and textures they choose. Each season is potent with reference points; even for people living in a climate that doesn't change dramatically from season to season, there are degrees of difference that have an impact on their fashion choices, whether they are the designers or the consumers.

What seasonal associations might someone make? Spring could bring showers and gardens to mind. Summer may evoke sunshine and sunflowers. Fall might conjure up a cavalcade of color as the leaves change. And winter has the potential to stir up frosty images of snow and ice. Although these are accurate reflections of spring, summer, fall, and winter, each designer has a unique set of variables that she brings to the table based on her personal experiences.

These fashion timelines are not simply linear. They are a set of parallel lines that begin at different points on the calendar. It's a balancing act for designers, because whichever season you're actually experiencing, as a fashion professional you are designing for at least two seasons ahead, producing for one season ahead, and delivering in the present day.

Below: Spring inspiration

Right: Colorful ensemble featuring floral embroidery by designer Nara Paz

Below: Summer inspiration

Right: Vintage hand-painted cotton dress from Poor Little Rich Girl

Below: Fall inspiration

Right: Copper leather shirt and satin stripe skirt by designer Elena Sanders

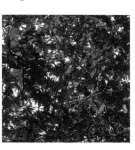

Below: Winter inspiration

Right: Black-and-white wool coat by designer Pavlina Gilson

38 Rote, Rules, and Roughs

A fashion designer may be tempted to avoid steps in the creative process to meet deadlines or simply reap the rewards a little sooner. Whether it's in sketching, patternmaking, or sewing, bypassing steps could undermine the final outcome.

- Sketching: A sense of the shape and flow of a garment can often initially be found in a rough sketch. Repeating that process on paper provides a place where details can be finessed before the actual garment is being developed.

- Patternmaking: Measure twice, cut once. Mathematics is a universal language, and there is little room for improvisation when it comes to accuracy. How pattern pieces interlock, how they are based on clear and detailed notations on a pattern, and how they adhere to the body's measurements are all based on a system of rules.

- Construction: Basting seems like the biggest waste of time, until something goes wrong. In the end, thinking about basting usually wastes more time than actually doing it. These temporary stitches serve much the same function as a rough sketch. They let you assess how the garment is coming together without taking permanent, and in some cases irreversible, steps.

In addition to getting it right the first time, each and every phase of preparation provides an opportunity for inspiration. The rules don't necessarily change, but the ones you apply, as well as how, when, and where you apply them, is a creative act in itself.

First stage of sketch: the rough

Middle stage(s) of sketch:
cleaning

Final stage of sketch:
color and detail

39 Hand to Eye

The connection between the mind's eye and the hands of the designer is easily taken for granted. This link must be reinforced through conscious exercise and exploration. If the communication between the two is fluid, a designer's dexterity in executing ideas becomes effortless and, after a time, second nature. Building strong bonds requires equal parts artist, architect, and construction worker. It's easy to play to your strengths, but a good designer will have a clear comprehension of cause and effect in every area.

A stitcher who understands how a pattern is designed to come together produces better work. The sequence of construction and detail placement will make a big difference in the finish of the final product.

The quality of a sketch is higher when it benefits from knowledge of construction techniques and experience with a wide variety of different fabrics. Rendering the roll of fabric cut on the bias has a distinctly different feel than drawing something cut on the lengthwise grain.

Patternmakers who can visualize how a garment will be sewn will be sure to include the right information in the pattern they're drafting. Including well-placed notches, the appropriate seam allowance, or enough ease is essential if the stitcher is going to be able to do his job well.

A designer should be able to navigate between visual mode where the imagination and aesthetics are paramount, the blueprint phase that documents and communicates how each design will be executed, and building something that respects and reflects the original vision and intent. The more direct the path between the designer's imagination and the realities of producing it, the better the work.

Above: Fashion sketch of a design by Victoria Dominguez-Bagu

Right: Design by Victoria Dominguez-Bagu

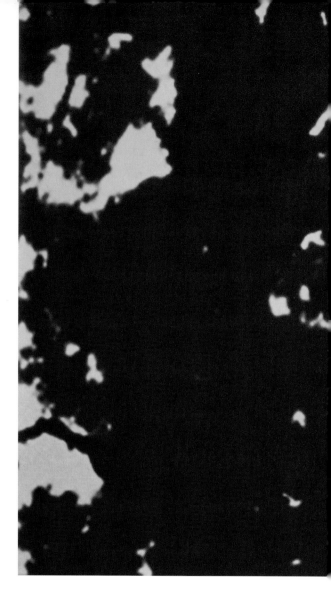

Right: Fashion sketch of a design by Victoria Dominguez Bagu

Far Right: Design by Victoria Dominguez-Bagu

40 Checks and Balances

One of the most important stages in the design process is self-correction. There may be a sense of something being off, but it's difficult to pinpoint the problem. To do this objectively, the piece needs to be taken out of context. There are several ways to check the work.

While rendering a two-dimensional representation of a design, turning the sketch upside down so that it can be seen as an abstract object helps to make imbalances obvious. A version of a sketch on tracing paper can be folded in half down the figure's center to avoid unwanted distortions.

The custom of working on the half is already practiced in patternmaking and draping because it cuts down on human error when trying to properly balance both sides of the garment. Even patterns for some asymmetrical garments can be started on the fold to ensure proper fit in areas that should reflect each other, allowing for the asymmetry to then be incorporated into the pattern.

When considering the fabrication of a design, colors should be checked in different types of light to have a clear vision of how the colors will read. Fabric should also be tested for transparency to avoid unwanted overexposure.

Throughout construction, double-checking seam allowance, dart lengths, and hems for consistency is a good practice to develop. Finishing hems that fall on the bias, like a circular skirt, should first be allowed to hang for at least twenty-four hours, because most fabric will end up sagging in those areas. This will allow the designer to ensure an evenly distributed skirt length.

Color in a fabric under natural light appears cool, with a blue cast.

Color in a fabric under incandescent light appears warm, with a red cast.

Color in a fabric under fluorescent light has a green cast.

When a tried-and-true basic sloper is used to generate a new pattern with an asymmetrical feature, starting the process on the fold will help ensure that the fit is consistent. Once the piece is opened and laid flat, almost any alteration to incorporate asymmetry into the new model can be made. The balance is already built in.

41 Machine Interface

The owner's manual will provide the fundamentals for using a sewing machine, but there is more to the relationship between sewer and machine than basic instructions. A successful interaction requires a commitment from the designer to "get to know" the machine. It's easy to attribute human characteristics, even personalities, to a machine that is used on a regular basis. Some designers develop such a strong bond that they go as far as naming their machines. This can be a good thing because it means the operator of that equipment is responsive to feedback she's getting. Audible, visual, and tactile clues unique to every machine help the sewer make decisions during the production process.

Although most sewing machines work in pretty much the same way, there are little differences and subtle nuances regarding how they work. Threading, bobbin type, power, and speed of the motor are a few of the most obvious things that will vary among machines.

If the designer is able to recognize machine parts and understand their function, she can solve problems more easily. A foot pedal, power cord, spool holder, bobbin winder, tension discs, stitch length, width and needle position adjustments, take-up lever, presser foot, pressure adjustment, throat plate, feed dog, hand wheel, motor, belt, thread cutter, slide plate, bobbin, and bobbin case are the parts common to most machines. Become intimately acquainted with your machine. Read the manual.

Cleaning, lubrication, and mechanical adjustments are a part of basic maintenance that ensures consistent results. Safe practices are often based on common sense. Don't rush, don't force, keep the area neat, and keep fingers away from the needle. If fabric is being fed into the machine properly, there is no reason why hands should ever be close enough to cause injury.

An investment of time and energy is required if designers are going to have a good experience and positive results.

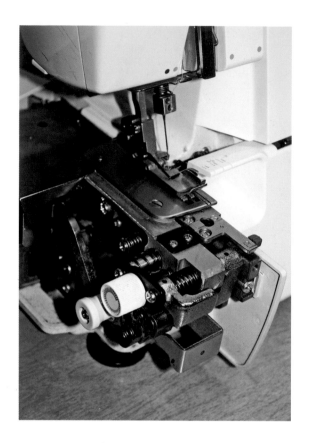

Inside an overlock machine

Inside a buttonhole machine

42 Cut, Drape, and Fold

Close examination of how fabric is manipulated by cutting, draping, and folding allows the designer to build subtle and dynamic elements into a design. Developing alternative cutting strategies, wrapping the figure in soft folds, or designing systems of pleats, permits the designer to transform any silhouette.

The role of the cutter in a design room seems simple enough—cut the pieces—but it is a job that demands great precision and attention to detail. How the garment is cut, especially when using patterned fabrics like stripes, checks, and plaids can result in different appearances. Pieces can be cut on different grains or the bias for effect.

There is a sensuality involved in draping fabric on and around the body. The sari (or saree) is an ideal example of a garment that uses artful draping. It is a length of fabric, approximately 5 to 10 yards (4.6 to 9.1 m) in length, usually featuring an ornamental border. It is not cut or sewn in any way. The contemporary sari is worn over a choli (sari blouse) and a petticoat. It can be draped in a variety of ways, but the Nivi style is the most popular.

Scottish tartans were originally draped in a fashion similar to the sari, called the Great Kilt, giving a soft toga-like appearance. The kilt has evolved over time to take on a more tailored look, featuring precisely measured and perfectly pressed knife or box pleats. The modern kilt uses 6 to 8 yards (5.5 to 7.3 m) of fabric and can be pleated to set, which although pleated, visually maintains the tartan repeat. A kilt can also be pleated to stripe, a method associated with kilts for the military. A proper tartan is made of wool twill and must be identical in both directions of the warp and weft of the fabric. Methods that require an adherence to the kind of rigid rules involved in kilt-making cultivate a beauty only mathematics can provide.

Kilt by Hector Russell, Edinburgh, Scotland

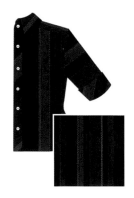

Straight-grain top
Straight-grain swatch

Bias top
Bias swatch

Cross-grain top
Cross-grain swatch

Vintage sari courtesy
of Shelley Chhabra

43 Underpinnings and Assembly

Any garment, from plain to intricate, will benefit from a sound infrastructure. Well-constructed garments rely on many elements that are not apparent at first glance. Good workmanship will depend upon specific techniques and additional materials that best serve the design.

Choosing the best seam for a project is contingent on the effect the designer is trying to achieve and the nature of the materials being used. Simple garments may use plain seams that can be finished with pinking shears or overlock stitching to prevent unraveling. Bound seams are finished with a strip of bias-cut fabric and are commonly found in unlined garments. A French seam is a seam within a seam, which works well with shear fabrics. Lapped or flat-felled seams can be found on jeans and are used for their strength and durability.

Facings are used to finish off areas such as a neckline or an armhole. Fusible and sew-in interfacings are found in facings, cuffs, collars, plackets, and buttonholes to add body, keep shape, and support and reinforce an area. They are available as woven, nonwoven, and knit materials.

Lining is the ideal way to professionally finish a garment. Interlining is used between the lining and the garment to provide warmth, whereas underlining is used to alter the hand (drape and feel) of the fabric, while also stabilizing and strengthening it. It can be as light as organza or as rigid as buckram.

Boning is another type of stabilizer and is not restricted to use in corsets, bustiers, and strapless cresses. It can be used along side seams to prevent sagging or as part of a neckline to avoid gaping. It can be applied to any area to prevent it from collapsing and taking away from the design.

Depending on the garment's design, there is always a logical order for its assembly. How it is assembled and finished also affects the final product. Which areas are to be stitched? Glued? Taped? Fused? Every choice takes the garment in a different direction, making it truly unique to the designer who conceived of it.

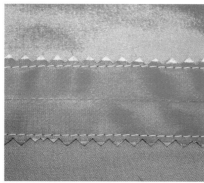
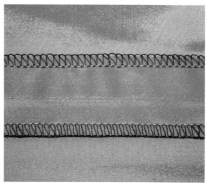

Clockwise: Boned bodice; Overlocked seam; Pinked seam

Infrastructure of a Daniel
Faucher Couture bridal gown

44 Manipulating Fullness

The volume and bulk of a garment can be controlled by various methods.

Gathering fabric is one way to add fullness. Ruffles are made of gathered fabric that is released on one edge. Shirring involves gathering on opposite edges, in multiple rows, so that the rows are contained. Both flounces, which are created using circular shapes, and godets—wedge-shaped inserts—are used to add flared fullness. Smocking involves pinching fabric in patterns such as the honeycomb. The silhouette of a garment can also be pumped up with quilting and stuffing.

Fabric can also be folded to create many different types of pleats that manage fullness. Flat pleats such as knife, fan, accordion, box, and inverted box can be pressed or unpressed, can be partial, or can run the full length of the area. Broomstick pleating is an irregular, crushed type of pleat. Examples of projecting pleats include cartridge, pinched, and tubular. Tucks can be spaced, graduated, doubled, and tapered, as well as being contoured, slashed, and cross-stitched. Materials that have a minimum of 60 percent man-made fiber have thermoplastic properties, which means they will retain shapes that are baked in with heat. These heat-treated fabrics are ideal for creating starburst pleating and variations on Fortuny-style pleating.

Darts are one of the most efficient ways to eliminate unwanted fullness and contour the shape of a garment. They are usually triangular or diamond shaped and sewn right sides together so that excess fabric can be folded or trimmed away.

Many of these techniques can be used in concert and the combinations are endless. Devising a plan for the application of any of these procedures can contribute to both silhouette and surface texture.

Above: Gathers create volume in a Christian LaCroix dress.

Right: Empire dress pleated at bust by Victoria Dominguez-Bagu

Box pleats are gathered into the bubble silhouette of a cocktail dress by Eddi Phillips.

45 Body Mapping

The leg bone's connected to the knee bone, the knee bone's connected to the thigh bone, the thigh bone's connected to the hipbone, and so on and so forth. These are the roads to the cartography of couture. A step further than anatomy, body mapping is about understanding the relationships between different areas of the body, the experience of the wearer, and the garment itself. The concept of body mapping relies on self-observation and self-inquiry. The designer has to gather the same kind of insight by communicating with his client.

Similar to using a road map, a body map anticipates needs to build in the structure, function, and size. Does a strapless dress have enough structural support to keep it from slipping down the body as the wearer moves? In the case of garments being used in active situations, do the garments allow for full articulations of joints, muscle reflexes, and/or how the body expands as it breathes? Is there enough ease in the seat of a garment that is worn by someone who sits most of the day? If the answer to any of these questions is "no," the designer can make course corrections while developing the garment that allow for efficient, elegant movement and comfort in any situation. These are all physical realities, but there are also abstract boundaries influenced by society and a designer's sensibilities, such as how low a neckline on a blouse can and should go.

① Designing a neckline close to the base of the neck should take into consideration that the neck naturally leans forward so as not to constrict the throat. The height of a collar may interfere with the head's range of motion.

② The shoulder is a pivot point for the arm. When engineering an armhole, the designer must consider how much ease will allow for full or limited rotation of the arm. The depth and breadth of the armhole will also be a contributing factor to fit.

③ The fit at the bustline must take into consideration not only the measurement and the cup size, but also the contraction and expansion of the lungs—which also affects the back. The back of the garment is subject to additional stress across the shoulder blades due to the natural tendency of the arms to reach forward.

④ The elbow is a primary stress point for a sleeve. A small dart at the elbow will allow the arm to bend without putting undue wear and tear on the sleeve while still retaining a snug fit. Adding volume to the sleeve at this point will also allow for freedom of movement, but alters the silhouette.

⑤ The height and shape of the rise in a pant must allow for any extension of the abdomen, the fullness and shape of the backside, and the fact that the body bends at this point. When the figure bends or sits, the seat spreads.

⑥ The knee is a primary stress point for the pant leg. The pant leg may be designed with a generous amount of ease to maintain a smooth silhouette or be intentionally lacking ease in order to create a shape that bunches up and grabs at the knee.

⑦ A pleat, a slit, or a wrap detail will allow for a full stride in a skirt with a narrow silhouette. The designer may limit movement by design to bring about a very specific way to move in the garment. Some examples include the traditional kimono or Paul Poiret's hobble skirt of the 1910s.

① ② ③ ④ ⑤ ⑥ ⑦

...ormity

Having been raised in India, where uniforms were a fact of life in public school, Sheena Matheiken had no problem pledging to wear the same dress for 365 days (seven identical dresses, one for each day of the week). The challenge lay in styling and restyling the dress so that no two days were the same. The whole project was developed as a fundraiser for Akanksha Foundation. The concept is a testament to putting a new face on how much we can do to express ourselves, even within the constraints of a uniform, simultaneously speaking to issues such as sustainability, while supporting a great cause.

In the arena of more traditional uniforms, these garments become symbols associated with the military, law enforcement, protection, rescue, and the service industry. Uniform design has its limits and may not have the glamour of trend-based designs, but the challenge comes in the form of professional standards of quality, comfort, durability, safety, and any of the specific requirements of the job.

Right: Beyond the practical there is the pageantry. Due to the historic and heroic nature of many of those who wear a uniform, there are often formal ceremonies that require a little more grandeur. This might be done gently with ribbons and/or with a great deal more impact, as in the case of the Scottish military tattoo where long-standing tradition dictates the flourish of details.

Below: Blauer police uniform details

Uniform Project dress

47 Fit

Garments can grab, skim, or bag around the wearer's body depending on the designer's aesthetic of fit. A flattering fit may be in the eye of the beholder, but as a rule, garments that squeeze and cut into the body, or that overwhelm it with volume, are not usually considered attractive or properly sized. Ultimately, opinions regarding fit are always subjective, due to a wide variety of cultural influences that cultivate different standards of beauty.

A tight fit will seize the body, becoming a second skin, often creasing and folding as it strains to cover the area.

A true fit will follow the contours of the body, using a balance of gentle tailoring and ease to retain the integrity of the silhouette.

A loose fit's generous proportions might also be considered relaxed or oversized because they allow for a full range of motion.

Other factors to consider when addressing the fit of a garment include vanity sizing, which more accurately reflects the psychology of the customer rather than her actual size. Category sizing, as in Misses, Junior, Women's, and Petite, are used to inform sizing for specific body types. There is really no such thing as one size fits all, because although you may be able to get a garment over your body, the fit will be different from person to person.

Customization is always an option when it comes to providing the proper fit for the customer, but designers can also develop in-house sizing standards that reflect specific body measurements. Armed with this useful tool, customers always know what they're getting.

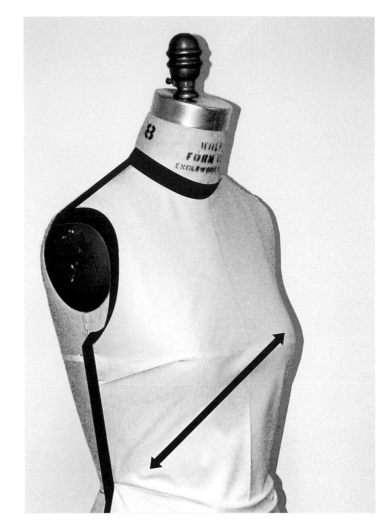

Tight fit

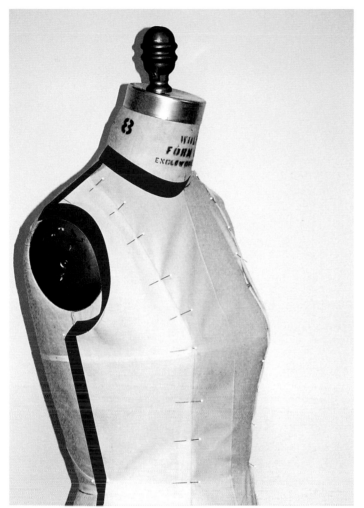

True fit

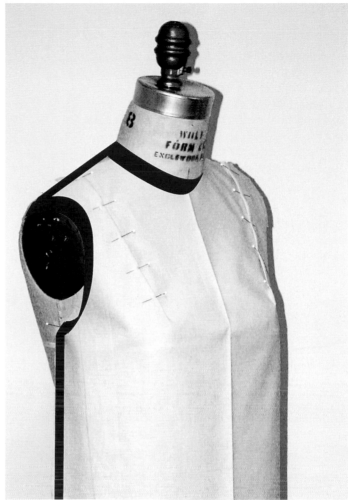

Loose fit

48 Mend and Alter

"Make Do and Mend" was the name of a campaign during World War II which encouraged the repair and repurposing of everything that still had the potential to be useful. Waste was the enemy, and this movement set a creative challenge to women everywhere to do their part and still be stylish. Booklets were distributed that included techniques such as binding frayed edges, darning, taking garments in and letting them out, recutting a garment into a new style, unpicking a knit, reknitting with the same yarn, and plain as well as decorative patching. Necessity became both the mother of invention and fashion.

Fixing imperfections is an exercise in finding the beauty in flaws. Even altering perfectly good garments can enhance the overall look and feel, and in the end can create a unique design for the wearer.

Make Do and Mend booklet

Left: Recut and repurposed brown plaid dress by Shannon Glasheen

1

2

3

1. Origin: gray knit hoodie sweatshirt

2. Origin: men's plaid flannel jacket

3. Origin: herringbone pencil skirt

Right: Recut and repurposed color blocked dress by Shannon Glasheen

4

5

6

4. Origin: men's red hoodie sweatshirt and women's terry cloth tank top

5. Origin: Vespa logo T-shirt

6. Origin: African dashiki

49 Deconstruct and Reconstruct

In the name of sustainability as well as style, many designers are taking unwanted clothes apart and refashioning them into completely different and original garments. In the interest of making good use of the mountains of discarded fashions that sit in closets, thrift stores, and warehouses around the globe—if they have not already been relegated to landfills—these designers transform the secondhand and the unsold into relevant new fashions. This repurposing resonates with a generation of fashion enthusiasts concerned with the environment.

Designer Shannon Glasheen applies all her training in patternmaking and construction to repurpose garments that may be outdated, well worn, or misunderstood. Breathing new life into pieces such as these requires that the designer look at each item as raw material and not as a finished product. Once dissected, there may also be very specific sections of a garment that can be reoriented to serve a new purpose. Building hybrids is another variation of this method, where elements from various garments are remixed into a designer mashup.

For designers working within the confines of a business model with different demands, the deconstruct/reconstruct approach to the design process can be incorporated as an aesthetic from the start, utilizing it to develop sample garments that can then be replicated.

Shannon Glasheen designs

PHOTOS: LINDSEY GLASHEEN-CRAWFORD

50 Structure and Scale

In the wild, when confronted by an animal, some experts suggest extending your arms over your head or out to your sides, or holding your jacket open, to give the impression of being larger and more threatening. Basic reptilian brain survival instincts might be at the core of what drives us to reframe our bodies to simulate more imposing shapes. A colorful example of fright or flight fashion can be found among the costumes designed by Tim Chappel and Lizzy Gardiner for the movie *Priscilla Queen of the Desert*. Many costume ideas for that film came from animal life indigenous to Australia. One of those creatures, the frill-neck lizard, has a ruff of skin around its neck that flares out when frightened. The designers emulated that feature to dramatic effect in a collar on one of the costumes. When the male peacock fans out its feathers to attract a mate, it creates a very different survival impulse.

The hoop skirt is an undergarment that consists of rigid concentric rings made of rope, osiers, whalebone, steel, or nylon, and suspended by fabric or bands of ribbon. When stored, the structure can collapse into itself, but when worn, the whole thing functions as a support system for a woman's skirt. Particular shapes reflect the fashion of any specific period, but the scale also provides a measure of personal space that keeps everyone at arm's length. The French word *panniers* refers to wicker baskets that are slung on either side of a pack animal. Panniers used for fashion were fastened onto a woman's hips to create an effect similar to the hoop skirt.

Headdresses, shoulder pads, bustles, and trains are also used to extend ourselves and our personal boundaries in the name of fashion. At a time when fashion was focused on the bust, Vivienne Westwood is credited with diverting us to the rear with bustles dubbed *Faux Cul*, that celebrated, if not exaggerated, a woman's derriere.

1

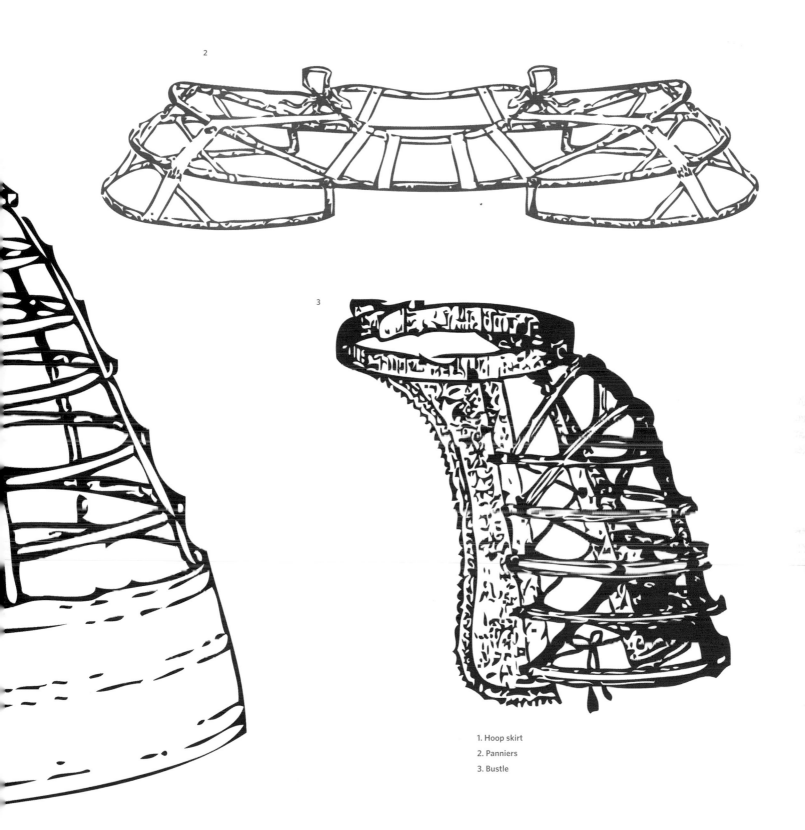

1. Hoop skirt

2. Panniers

3. Bustle

51 Anatomically Correct

It is no coincidence that one of the things that designer Geoffrey Beene is known for is liberating a woman's body. He studied medicine at Tulane University for three years before shifting gears and studying fashion at Traphagen School of Fashion. He understood the mechanics of the body, and therefore eliminated conventional impediments such as unnecessary padding, interlinings, zippers, and fasteners.

Comfort is one of the primary concerns for the contemporary consumer. A designer benefits from understanding the body and how it works, such as what happens when a muscle contracts, relaxes, or extends. Will a garment provide unrestricted movement? Structures that encase the body need to respond to the pliability of muscles and the rigidity of bones. Studying the anatomy of mammals, birds, insects, reptiles, and aquatic life could provide a wealth of design cues. The architecture of plant life might suggest alternative methods in solving creative challenges. Even microscopic organisms can serve as a source of inspiration.

Athletic garments, medical garments, and undergarments take advantage of textile technology and engineering to address the issues associated with mobility. Beyond range of motion, the same tools can be applied to compressing the body to protect or reshape it. A good comprehension of the body and how it works also allows the designer to isolate aspects of the design process to address specific areas of the body, with each zone offering its own advantages and disadvantages.

Haute Contour, the Dessert Shapewear™ by SPANX, launched in 2009 is the next step in the evolution of foundation garments, designed to achieve a specific silhouette while also providing gentler support and more comfort than it's predecessors—the corset and the girdle. What may be initially taken for granted as a simple undergarment is now infused with the kind of scientific research and technology that make it a powerful partner in the process of fashion design.

52 Roads Less Traveled

A designer who focuses primarily on the front torso when designing a garment is missing out on an opportunity to explore and accentuate other parts of the body. Here are other important areas to consider:

Going Below
For some designers, the lower half of the garment or ensemble is an afterthought, something that completes the look but remains secondary and subordinate to the top. The hem of a dress, an embellishment on a skirt, and the shape of a pant all have just as much power to set the tone for the rest of the outfit.

From Behind
Making an entrance is one thing, but how someone looks as she turns and walks away has the potential to have as much impact, if not more so. Plunging backs, skirt tails, bows, flowers, and other flourishes are just a few of the ways to bring up the rear.

Side to Side
The satin trim down the side seam of a tuxedo pant is not the extent of detail that can be placed in this area. The very seam itself provides myriad choices. Side seams can split to reveal, pleat to control fullness, incorporate a closure, or be decorated.

Inside Look
Close and careful attention to the workmanship and special details inside a garment are the mark of a fine product.

Right: Kira McClellan side detail

Below: Valentino back detail

Far Right: Aey Hotarwaisaya design with focus on skirt hem detail

53 Camouflage and Complement

When it comes to camouflaging or complementing the shape of a body, designers need to think about how to conceal or accentuate differences in body shape. A designer who treats these deviations from the average like variations and not flaws is already a step ahead in the psychology of fashion. Consider that average is just a reference point. It usually indicates balanced proportions in a scale that relates to height, width, and weight. These basic body types benefit from special design details:

The Apple
Broad shoulders and narrow hips can benefit from something that breaks up the width of the shoulder, such as a halter neckline.

The Pear
Emphasizing the torso, especially the shoulders, and downplaying the hips will balance a frame with narrow shoulders and a fuller hip.

The Ruler
The combination of narrow shoulders and hips creates a long, thin frame. That length can be broken up with horizontal lines as well as cups or other detail that enhances the bustline.

The Hourglass and the Fuller Figure
Broad shoulders, full bust, and full hips benefit from asymmetrical style lines. If the midsection is fuller, details such as ruching can create the illusion of a more tapered waistline.

Adding other factors into the equation, such as long waist, short waist, cup size, height, and weight, gives rise to nuances that may require adjustments and/or adaptations. Cut, length, style lines, asymmetry, detail placement, padding, and corseting are some of the design choices that assist in the modification of a body type through clothing. Transforming the appearance of a figure is about redirecting attention, and not about correction.

Clockwise:
Bathing suit drawings: apple; pear; ruler; hourglass

54 Clothes That Carry

Whether it is the smallest of five pockets on a pair of jeans meant for spare change, or a large pouch on the front of a hooded sweatshirt, any type of pocket can be equal parts function and design. Even an in-seam pocket, which is meant to disappear, helps to keep the lines of the design smooth while simultaneously providing the capacity to carry.

World War II is recognized as a period in which many technological advances were made in response to the demands of the day. Designs developed during that era also reflected needs unique to the time period, as is evident in the creation of the kangaroo cloak. This garment was designed with huge pockets that allowed the wearer to quickly stuff them with household items when air raid sirens went off.

Pockets can do double duty depending on how they're made and what they're made of. Some pockets can be turned inside out to envelop a garment, like a windbreaker or rain poncho. When made out of fleece, they can serve as hand warmers in outerwear.

Designing practical pockets for carpenter pants will be dictated by the specific tools that need to be carried. Any type of pocket can have a flap that is fastened by buttons or Velcro. Zipper pockets offer another type of closure. Pockets can be inserted into a slit in the fabric and embellished/strengthened with a welt.

Accessories that act as utility belts, such as the fanny pack, pocket belts, bum bags, or hip sack, are popular for their versatility. Clothing developed for the military or special activities, such as safari jackets, fishing vests, and photography vests, provides templates for pocket-driven design. The cargo pant is standard issue in the armed forces, as well as in many fashionable wardrobes.

Patch pocket with button flap

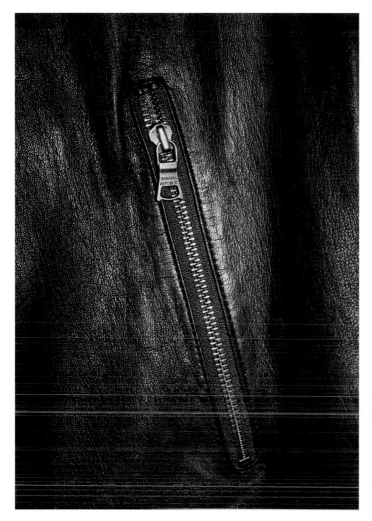

Inset zipper pocket

Inset welt pocket

55 Design unto Others

Design unto others as you would have them design unto you. This golden rule should always be referenced during the design process, especially in the world of fashion. What are the customer's concerns when it comes to clothing? A designer must develop a certain level of empathy for clients who place different demands on the apparel they purchase.

Put yourself in the place of someone who is especially tall, petite, thin, or full-figured, or whose body proportions have unexpectedly changed dramatically. In addition to the psychological concerns, there are undeniable physical aspects to contend with.

Fashion design for the elderly is an important consideration as well. As we get older, our sensitivity to changes in temperature and texture increases. Limited mobility is also considered a factor.

Disabilities that require the use of a cane, walker, or wheelchair provide the designer with perceptible issues that must be addressed. Arthritis is a disability that is less obvious. Button closures that might seem simple enough at first glance could pose a challenge for someone living with arthritis. Possible solutions can be found in the most unpredictable places. The long zipper pull for the back zipper on a wetsuit might be one way to deal with a back zipper on a dress for someone with limited range of motion.

Fashion designers can take a cue from other industries that have incorporated these principles into their work as benchmarks of good design. For example, the mission of the Institute for Human Centered Design is to expand and enhance experiences for people of all ages and abilities through design to improve quality of life. Designers who can put themselves in the shoes of any of these clients will develop sensibilities that influence and enhance their work.

Wetsuit zipper detail

PHOTO: ERIK ISAKSON/GETTY IMAGES

When honoring fashionable and elder clientele, a designer may find inspiration in the form of the iconic American model Carmen Dell'Orefice, who began her career at the age of fifteen in 1946 and continues to be a sought-after model on the runways and in print. With the muse of maturity, designers can counteract the ageism of the fashion industry and truly serve their customer. Grandmothers are no longer relegated to their rocking chairs—instead they can be found at the gym on the treadmill beside you—not to mention the front row.

56 Reshape and Reconfigure

Once of the easiest ways to reshape a garment is to belt it. Whether it serves to grab and control volume or create a visual break, the effect is powerful. Consumers are looking for versatility in their wardrobes and designers can build that versatility into their work by considering how tying off a garment at different places will transform it.

Contrasting belts create the most obvious break. A self-belt is a softer way to cinch a shape. Drawstrings do the same job but can be discreetly hidden within channels positioned almost anywhere on a garment—under the bust, within side seams, at the waist, along the sleeve, or on pant legs and skirt hems.

Silhouettes can also be transformed when parts of the garment can be attached or removed with button, zip, snap, hook, or Velcro. Sleeves button off and transform a jacket into a vest. Pant legs zip off to become shorts. A snap-on peplum will take a day jacket into evening. A skirt or train can be bustled up with hidden hooks. Shoulder pads Velcro in to create an exaggerated shape. Even bulk can be adjusted with removable linings.

Viktor & Rolf belted trench coat

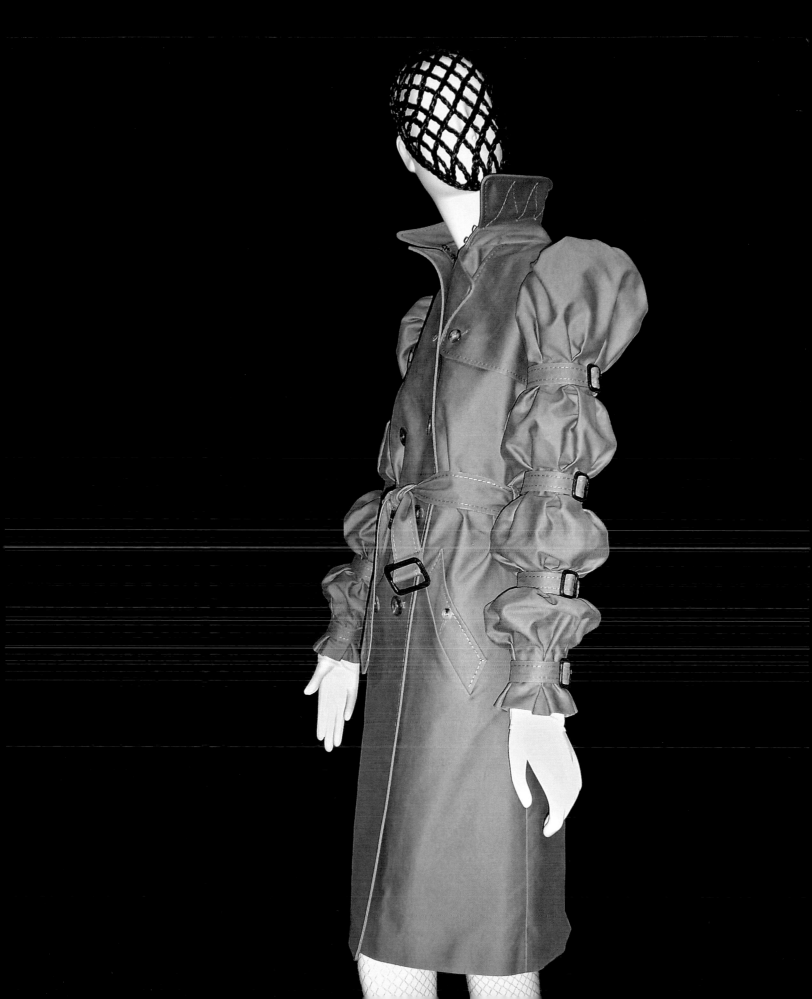

57 Resurface

The imaginative application of decorative couture details allows for even the most modest of fabrics to become extraordinary. The use of thread, beads, sequins, flowers, appliqué, feathers, and ribbon is largely a decorative process that involves raw materials that are not necessarily generated by the original cloth. Using only the fabric itself, it is also possible to transform both the surface and the silhouette with ruching, bustles, quilting, ruffles, and pickups. The ability to alter, emphasize, and accent a concept is restricted only by one's imagination.

Beading

Embroidery

Fabric roses

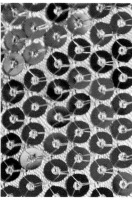

Sequins

Feathers

Corded appliqué

Quilting

Gold sequin dress by
Daniela Corte

58 A Cut Above

Scissors are an essential part of a designer's tool kit, for obvious reasons. When it comes to most garments, a designer will use shears to trim away excess fabric and shape the overall silhouette, which includes carving out necklines and arm-holes. The laser takes the art of the cut to a new level of precision and efficiency.

Although cutting holes and trimming edges into scallops is technically a process of elimination, it is also a form of decoration. Shaped keyhole openings have long been incorporated into the design of a closure, but these openings can be scaled and even multiplied for dramatic effect. The cutaway aesthetic is also the basis of cut-work needle lace and embroideries. The edges of any area that is extracted may be left untreated, bound with thread, or finished with a facing. Carefully considered cutting proves that there are times when what is removed is as important as what is added.

PHOTO BY FRANCOIS GUILLOT/AFP/GETTY IMAGES

A model wearing a ready-to-wear outfit featuring cut-outs by designer Yohji Yamamoto, 2010

A model wearing a cut-out ensemble from Jean-Charles de Castelbajac's ready-to-wear collection, 2006

59 Fringe and Fray

The outer edges of a silhouette need not be the definitive finish line of a garment. Deliberately adding some type of trim to the edge of a garment will have a more organic and less rigid quality. Fringe softens a shape by eliminating the hard line by way of movement, and in some instances, irregular lengths. Pompoms, tassels, beads, and feathers have all been used to create interesting and playful edges. Even simple eyelash fringe on a flapper-inspired dress will dance on the surface of the design with just the slightest of movements. Such an animated garment is compelling and entertaining.

A word of caution is in order for designers who see frayed edges as an easy out from the traditional and often challenging work of finishing a garment. Incorporating a raw edge into a garment has its own set of challenges if it is to be done well. If the grain line at that edge is not properly aligned, it will end up fraying unevenly. If the fabric is prone to fraying, it's imperative to apply a stay stitch to control how far it will unravel. Natural frayed edges will soften and relax even the most iconic of tailored garments, such as a Chanel suit.

Dress by Aida Lourenco with frayed hem as the center of interest

A model in fringed white suit
by Chanel, 2005

Add, Subtract, and Preserve

A sculptor is afforded three basic processes that will inform the style of the final work. She may add, subtract, or preserve. A designer approaches the use of materials in much the same way. Each has an impact on the spatial relationship of a garment to the wearer as well as the environment that surrounds it.

Lady Gaga is known for her high-concept fashion sense, taking inspiration from avant-garde designers such as Martin Margiela and Alexander McQueen. Part of her haute couture trousseau includes variations of a dress inspired by Thierry Mugler. The design of the dress features multifaceted three-dimensional shapes that project from her body like an explosion of crystal stalagmites. Costumes like these use the additive process, assembling the final shape by building onto a core garment.

The tulle gowns in a Viktor & Rolf 2010 collection achieved a level of surrealism that would have impressed Salvador Dali. The meticulously carved silhouettes were an exercise in the creation of negative space. These carefully executed voids defy comprehension and leave most asking, "How did they do that?" The Dutch design team assured environmental watchdogs that the missing fabric was properly recycled.

In the art of origami, nothing is removed or added. Only through folding does the form take and retain its shape. The Marc Jacobs collection for Dior in 2007 experimented with the life-size application of folds and pleating used in origami. The gowns were obviously not constructed from one altered piece of square fabric, but the draping and surface treatments do pay homage to the graceful forms that result from thoughtful folding.

Lady Gaga in a three-dimensional black and gold dress, 2008

A model in an origami-inspired gown from the Christian Dior Haute Couture Collection, Spring/Summer 2007

PHOTO BY LARRY MARANO/GETTY IMAGES

PHOTO BY ERIC RYAN/GETTY IMAGES

A model wearing a sculptural cut-out gown by Viktor & Rolf, 2010

Change Agents

Clever couture that is multifunctional by design is not only a great investment, but also a creative exercise for both the designer and the user. One example is a gown designed by Norma Kamali, exclusively for eBay. It can be worn in several different ways: boatneck, one-shoulder, strapless, halter, and cross-halter evening gown, all in one. Belted and bloused, the gown transforms into a dress for everyday. Some designers, such as Karolina Zmarlak, are making the concept of convertible clothing a part of their brand DNA.

Athletic garments and clothing meant for outdoor activities often benefit from being versatile as well. Being able to pull a drawstring, button on a hood, or zip off a pant leg allows the user to respond to a situation in short order. The novelty of these very practical applications makes them an attractive design detail to incorporate into other categories of fashion. More often these adoptions are more about aesthetics than function.

Advances in the science of dyes include UV-reactive photochromic paints, which change color in the sun and glow under a black light. When these paints are used in thread, fabrics, and beads, clothes can take on a life of their own depending on their environment. In the hands of innovator Hussein Chalayan, the technology of change is more complex. The designer's collection of transformer dresses pushed the boundaries of fabrication with the help of the London-based engineering firm 2D:3D. Computer systems built into the garment mechanically morphed it into a different shape and style without any external assistance. Inter-industry partnerships like this one make it possible for a designer's creativity to reach new heights.

Norma Kamali convertible dress versions

TECHNICAL DRAWINGS BY MARIE-EVE TREMBLAY

Left: Karolina Zmarlak convertible design versions

Below: A model wearing a garment that transformed into a different silhouette using technology by designer Hussein Chalayan, 2007

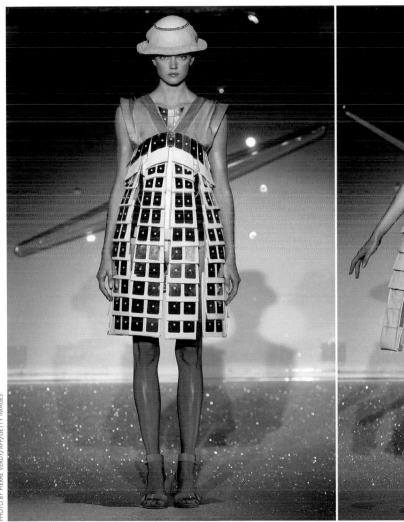
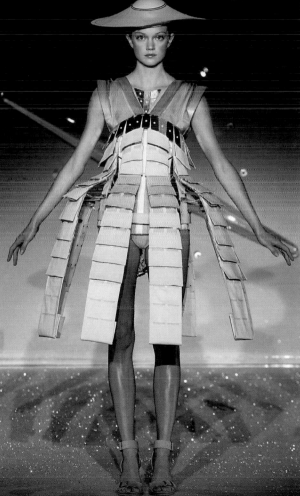

Drawing the Eye

The designer is in the driver's seat when it comes to mapping a path for the eye to travel. A sense of movement can be achieved with repeating patterns as well as the variations in those patterns that create rhythm. Action or implied action in the form of anything that points in a specific direction may use a graduation of sizes, color, or intensity. The fashion designer can control where to place elements that block or push in and around the body. Emphasis will dominate the composition and arrest attention. Equal billing cancels everything out; with no focal point, the overall design is unremarkable. Careful observation and meticulous application of potential focal points allow designers to control the pulse of their design. Where does the eye linger? What makes it dart away?

Eddi Phillips' silver cocktail dress uses color and embellishment to create a powerful focal point.

63 A-Symmetry

Symmetry and balance are not necessarily the same things. Symmetry is defined by sides that mirror each other. In this case, the balance would be considered formal. Symmetry can also be achieved through radial balance where all elements radiate from a central focal point.

An informal balance can be found in design that is asymmetrical, like a one-shouldered gown. When one side does not reflect the other, there is an absence of symmetry and a designer must rely on instinct and experience to find the right harmony. With each side working independently, it is important to build relationships between the dissimilar—vibrant color and neutral color; dark, light, and mid-tones; flat and three-dimensional; small and large; a variety of shapes; position and relative placement; or solid and pattern.

Whether through symmetry or asymmetry, the designer can draw deliberate attention to an area by directing the observer with arrow-shaped/triangular objects. Zigzags are another way to take command of the viewer. As a rule, the bias can be a powerful tool because of the energy and disruptive nature of the diagonal line.

A test of balance in symmetrical or asymmetrical garments is to gauge how focused the observer's attention is. If the viewer's eye travels around the piece, taking in the whole, there is an indication of balance. Even a seemingly chaotic dispersal of details can achieve balance if there is an overall sense of unity. Many balanced couture compositions, but not all, tend to be visually weighted or stabilized at the bottom of the piece.

Right: Pavlina Gilson layers an asymmetrical design over a symmetrical day dress.

Below: Maison Martin Margiela vest featuring leather straps, woven into an asymmetrical pattern

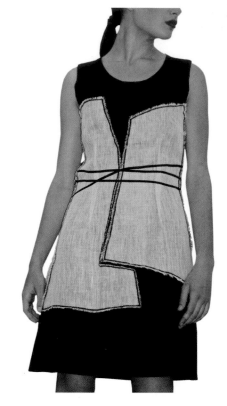

Samira Vargas ensemble

64 Intarsia: Puzzles and Missing Links

Solving a mystery can be an irresistible challenge—so much so that we will create them ourselves to stimulate our minds. Designers can use the principles of puzzle making to test their problem-solving skills. If a designer can successfully express his ideas in a more complex fashion, those intricacies have the potential to captivate the imaginations of others. Patternmaking is, in essence, one big mathematical puzzle.

The nonogram is a puzzle akin to mosaics, which is the art of creating patterns and pictures by assembling small pieces of colored material. Once the designer designates the particular placement of color, it becomes paint by numbers until the final picture is revealed. The process usually involves squares or other specific geometric shapes, but architect Antoni Gaudí used the angles and curves he observed in nature to create his very unique and organic mosaics. Pieced work or patchwork is an example of how this technique can be applied to fabric.

Computer displays employ the same principles of mosaics, because this medium is based on grids and utilizes small rectangles of color called pixels to build digital images. Photomosaics is an interesting alternative to this process, which uses photographs instead of solid blocks of color. To create multicolor patterns in knits, each new color is introduced by literally tying in a different yarn, but each stitch corresponds to the pixel principle. This technique is called intarsia. Cloth is woven by interlacing warp and weft threads. The combination of specific weaving patterns and carefully chosen colors can be used in much the same way.

A designer can connect the dots for her audience or intentionally tease. Providing you with all but one clue, the question becomes "What is X?" Obvious omissions are able to build curiosity around couture. Coded messages, and hidden meanings, entertain a designer's audience by allowing them to solve the cipher.

Peter Hidalgo dresses

65 The Reveal

Director Alfred Hitchcock integrated a personal cameo appearance into his films. Caricaturist Al Hirschfeld incorporated *Nina*, his daughter's name, into most of his drawings. Both became almost as famous for these veiled gifts as for the fine work they produced. Software, music, books, art, and television shows are just a few of the media where "Easter eggs" can be hidden. This long-standing tradition of weaving in special hidden surprises can also be found in fashion, with discovery becoming as much a part of the experience as the actual clothing.

There are some traditional target areas for the placement of a hidden treat. Classic shirts might hide them on the underside of the collar, the collar stand, or the inside cuff. Some sort of decorative detail might also be placed on the shirttail. Addressing the part of the tradition that requires "something blue," a bridal gown can be designed to include tiny blue bows sewn into the lining. A simple summer dress can make good use of a contrasting fabric to face the neckline, armhole, or hem of the garment, hinting at something more playful. The ambiguously playful message "Lucky You" can be found on a label placed on the inside zipper of Lucky Brand jeans.

Private moments and public displays of design can be carefully crafted into any garment. Letting your hand sink into a pocket lined with the softest fleece is a personal present from the designer to the wearer. A flashy lining in an otherwise conservative suit allows the user to choose when, where, and to whom he wishes to expose his wilder side to a real "Ta-da!" moment.

Right: Jeff Lahens for ECC Life & Style; undercollar detail

Middle: Arnold Scaasi dress with matching coat lining

Below: Sara Marhamo cuff lining detail

Jeff Lahens for ECC Life & Style; suit lining detail

66 Cultivated Influence

Fashion mavericks are commonly defined by a singular attribute: They followed their own instincts regardless of the conventions of their times. Marlene Dietrich and Katherine Hepburn have become reference points for the pant and menswear-inspired fashions for women—Dietrich in a top hat and tails, and Hepburn in casual suiting. In light of the history of pants for women, these ladies displayed a certain level of fashion bravery. Amelia Jenks Bloomer, an early advocate of women's rights in the United States, is known in part for adopting the fashion of wearing loose trousers gathered at the ankle. Ahead of its time, the trend did not last.

World War II made wearing pants a practical necessity for women who were working in factories, but it was not until the 1970s that slacks became a fashionable item to include as part of a woman's wardrobe. Designers tapped into the Women's Liberation Movement, infusing their collections with the all-empowering pant, which had become yet another symbol of equality between the sexes.

There are few contemporary examples of similar nonconformists. But there are more theatrical fashion renegades, such as Lady Gaga and Björk, who without question integrate fashion as part of their personalities that also translates to their performances. The question for designers who lean toward the rebellious is, "Which visionaries of style influence the essence of who you are as a designer?"

Right: Actress Marlene Dietrich making her Hollywood film debut as the tuxedo-clad Amy Jolly in the film *Morocco*, directed by Josef von Sternberg, 1930

Far Right: Portrait of actress Katharine Hepburn in slacks

PHOTO BY EUGENE ROBERT RICHEE/JOHN KOBAL FOUNDATION/GETTY IMAGES

PHOTO BY ALFRED EISENSTAEDT/TIME LIFE PICTURES/GETTY IMAGES

67 Curated Experience

It's a bird! It's a plane! It's a supermodel! The power of a fashion concept can be traced back to the most unexpected of sources. Who would have ever thought that an entire exhibition exploring the influences of superheroes on fashion would be the basis for an exhibition at the Metropolitan Museum of Art in New York? The "Superheroes: Fashion and Fantasy" exhibit filtered fashion through the colorful fiction of comic books and graphic novels. Beyond secret identities, the exhibition established specific strategies for creating superhero personas that had a direct correlation to fashion.

The fashion tactics employed included using graphics to brand a superhero; wrapping a hero in the flag to capitalize on patriotism; supersizing muscle to overemphasize the masculine or feminine strength; the contradiction of good and bad existing simultaneously within the same character; adding a protective layer of armor; how aerodynamic design feeds the need for speed; breaking with conventional standards of beauty; heroes that morphed into human-animal hybrids; and the introduction of the antihero, with a darker, grittier side that defied easy classification. This wealth of resources was generated from just one genre. Approaching fashion design like a museum curator has the advantage of being exposed to connections that may not have been obvious, and building a concept around that.

In "Superheroes: Fashion and Fantasy," the Costume Institute at the Metropolitan Museum of Art in New York explores fashionable superheroes. Outfits by designer Bernhard Willhelm and House of Moschino.

PHOTO BY STAN HONDA/AFP/GETTY IMAGES

68 Culture Filter

Anyone who hears the word *poncho* has an immediate image in her mind of what it is. The poncho was used very strategically in *Ugly Betty*, a television sitcom that revolved around the fashion world and a Mexican American family. Historically, the poncho has never really been able to gain a foothold as a definitively fashionable garment, but it does have a direct connection to Mexican folk culture. One of the first times the character of Betty Suarez is on-screen within the context of the fashion world, she is wearing a decidedly Mexican poncho. If we weren't certain of its origin, the word *Guadalajara* emblazoned across the front of it informs us immediately. There is also an interplay with a very glamorous character who is wearing a designer's interpretation of a poncho that brings the point home that Betty is not stylish. Used as a storytelling tool in entertainment, a stereotype straddles the border between humor and good taste, and that is exactly the same line that designers must be conscious of navigating when embracing cultural symbols as part of their concept.

Some designers shy away from incorporating elements from their own cultural background because they fear being stereotyped. Others avoid any direct cultural references because they cannot see beyond the folk costume. A designer must stretch, reaching beyond the expected, but not bypass the ethnic and cultural symbolism associated with the garment. Fashion can use the idea of a stereotype as a starting point, and let the idea evolve into a completely new expression of the source.

Inuit poncho from Iris Apfel private collection

America Ferrera stars as Betty Suarez in ABC Television's *Ugly Betty*.

69 More Is More

If a designer is able to synthesize a wide variety of elements into one garment, it has the potential to be a must-have, goes-with-everything garment. This type of core wardrobe item can be used as a fountainhead that branches out into a broad collection. But the designer must approach the design of each item with a greater understanding of how it works within the whole. This additive process should always enhance and never overwhelm, because the overall silhouette can easily be compromised by bulk.

Several strategies can be employed when assembling ensembles that involve many layers:

- Base layers should always be lighter than those on the next level.

- Concentrate on short over long, restricting the application to just one area—tanks over tees or leggings over tights, but not both.

- Control the visible proportions of each layer to see the shape it creates, and allow the eye to follow each layer.

- Select special items for the mix that are strong enough to stand alone.

- Draw attention to family resemblances in similar items and create the illusion of familiarity with dissimilar ones.

- Mix day into evening and bring a little nighttime glamour into the daylight.

- Coordinate looks that are comfortable and not forced.

Sara Marhamo design

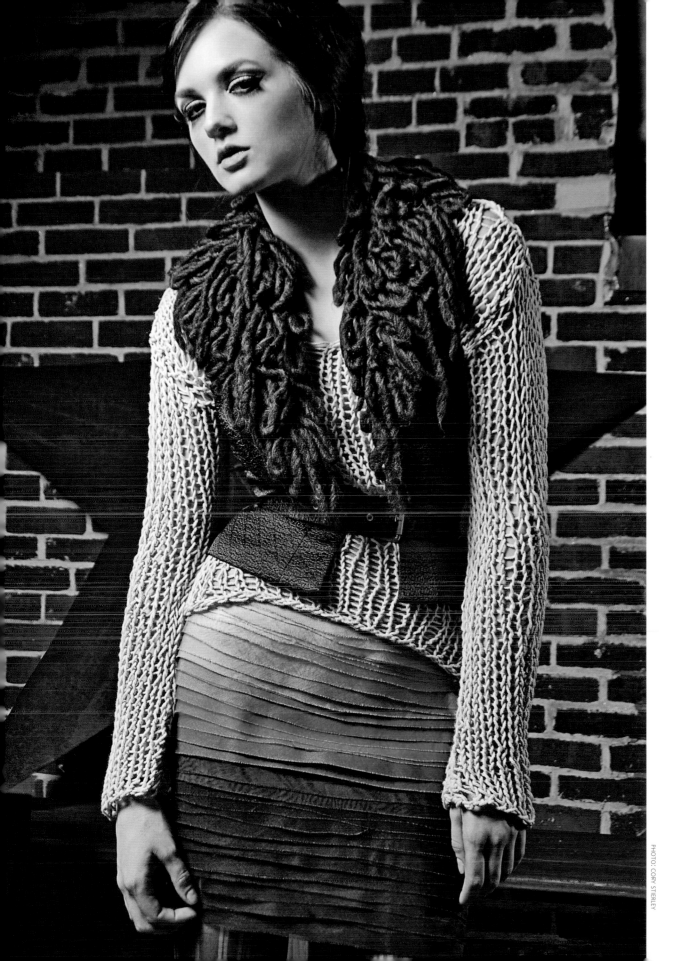

70 Less Is More

Ockham's razor is a principle that means "All things being equal, the simplest solution is usually the right one." As it relates to fashion, this rule of thumb sets the tone for designers who don't wish to embellish or complicate their work. Knowing when to stop is not always easy. A well-edited collection need not be austere and is strengthened by the power of minimalism. Designers must resist the temptation to add elements in order to disguise mistakes—a pitfall not uncommon among new designers. Be willing to start over. A designer should be able to create something simple and restrained that is as compelling as a more complex design.

Every designer should view his work through the visual filter of simplicity to avoid weighing ideas down with unnecessary clutter. Clear comprehension of the design challenge at hand allows the designer to emphasize the vital essentials. Anything that distracts should be revisited and, in many instances, discarded. But how many layers of design can be stripped away without compromising the garment's functionality or aesthetic value? When in doubt, leave it out.

Minimalist white dress by Donna Karan

PHOTO: JOEL BENJAMIN

on on a Dress

...d religious influences in fashion
...ent cultures and are often
...ainstream by bold, visionary
...instance, Madonna initiated a
trend for wearing crucifixes and rosary beads in
the 1980s. Jean Paul Gaultier showed a collection
in 1993 that was inspired by the traditional garments worn by Hasidic Jews. Religious iconog-
raphy also plays a big part in fashion. Christian
Lacroix ended his 2009 haute couture show
with a heavily embroidered gown that could be
described as a tribute to the Virgin Mary.

Internationally recognized figures such as the
Dalai Lama expose the globe to a way of life and
dress that people might not otherwise be aware
of. One example is the saffron robes of Tibetan
Buddhists. Along the same lines, many websites
are devoted to Hijab-friendly fashion for Muslim
women who wish to express their faith without
inhibiting their fashion sense. Exploring religion
through fashion can be seen as a tribute to all the
meaningful traditions, rich history, and beautiful
artwork associated with religion.

His Holiness the 14th Dalai
Lama in Tokyo, 2009

PHOTO BY KIYOSHI OTA/GETTY IMAGES

A model wearing a haute couture gown with distinctive religious references by designer Christian Lacroix, 2009

72 Building on Basics

Tried-and-true basics may feel like fallback items in fashion, but garments in this category exist because everyone understands and appreciates their value. Staple garments are not an easy out, because they actually pose greater challenges for the designer. Coming up with something completely different is often easier than putting your stamp on a classic.

The little black dress is a garment that most women own or have owned during their lifetime—it never goes out of style. It has been at the center of everything from museum exhibitions to morning-show makeovers. The first association most people make regarding the little black dress is through the film *Breakfast at Tiffany's* in which Audrey Hepburn wears one designed by Hubert de Givenchy. In fact, it is Gabrielle Coco Chanel's work in the 1920s that is credited as the origin of the modern-day little black dress. *Vogue* called it "Chanel's Ford," referring to the Model T, which was also designed to be simple and accessible. One of its most redeeming qualities is the ability to accessorize it to suit any occasion. For men, the tuxedo is a fashion staple for formal occasions, though most men don't actually own one. Defining the basics that a designer will include in her body of work requires as much, if not more, research and development if the designer wants her vision to be memorable.

PHOTO BY HULTON ARCHIVE/GETTY IMAGES

British actor and comedian Cary Grant in a tuxedo, 1953

A model wearing a sequined little black dress at a Marc Jacobs fashion show, 2010

73 Design of Dissent

Rebels have always influenced fashion. By today's standards, the flapper look of the 1920s is charming and chic. Nostalgia now clouds how women who epitomized that look were perceived, such as Louise Brooks and Clara Bow, who were the bad girls of their day. Rebellious and reckless, these girls bobbed their hair and wore flimsy dresses that exposed their knees and bared their arms.

Jean Harlow, Mae West, Joan Crawford, and Bette Davis personified the sloe-eyed vamp of the 1930s who broke with conventional morals and brandished overt sexuality in slinky satin gowns. Actresses such as Lana Turner, Virginia Mayo, and Barbara Stanwyck brought the femme fatale of the 1940s to life in film noir.

The undercurrent of the very conservative 1950s was part teenager, part Beat Generation, and part "rebel without a cause." Jeans and leather jackets were the major fashion influence of icons such as James Dean and Marlon Brando. Hippie fashions of the 1960s were heavily influenced by a bohemian lifestyle and the music of performers such as Joan Baez and Joni Mitchell. Punk is one of the most aggressive antifashion movements. In the 1970s, infamous performers such as Johnny Rotten and Sid Vicious of the Sex Pistols were dressed by Vivienne Westwood, who incorporated BDSM gear, safety pins, razor blades, and spiked dog collars into her fashions.

In direct contrast to slick power dressing in the 1980s, street fashion and deliberately torn clothing became the alternative fashion, heavily influenced by pop stars Madonna and Cindy Lauper. The 1980s also initiated the start of Goth, which has diversified over the years to include everything from horror to high fashion. Function trumped form in grunge fashions of the 1990s, popularized by the Seattle music scene, and in particular, Kurt Cobain. Layers of baggy, unkempt plaid flannel shirts, charity shop finds, cardigans, and combat boots comprised the look.

Fashion designers must be in touch with the fringes of fashion. Who are the outsiders of today that might be defining our era?

Goth-influenced style

PHOTO: JOEL BENJAMIN

Grunge-influenced style

74 Attitude Adjustment

Clothes do make the man, or the woman, when they are part of the storytelling process on stage or on-screen. Wardrobing successfully for film or the theater requires that each character is profiled accurately. For a costumer, understanding the character's history, psychology, circumstances, and environment is as important as a fashion designer's grasp of a client's lifestyle. Both rely on excellent powers of observation. Fashion tells a story as well. That tale is a hybrid of the designer's vision and the wearer's interests and eccentricities.

Many high-profile models build a career by establishing a distinct look that designers want to align themselves with, but models that are able to be chameleons will be valued for their ability to transform into the ideal of any client. Über-versatile supermodels of the 1980s, such as Linda Evangelista, were known as chameleons. They made good use of cosmetics, hairstyles, and clothes to transform their appearance in any fashion fantasy.

Fashion designers often cite films and actors as sources of their inspiration. Why not weave a story, based on a film or motivated by characters, into the fabric of a collection? Who is the muse du jour? What is she doing? Where is she going? How will she express herself? Getting into her head allows the designer to adjust and adapt the details of his work so that it hints at the source, but to avoid clichés, the designer must be able to pull the illusion into the context of reality.

PHOTO BY JEAN-PIERRE MULLER/AFP/GETTY IMAGES

Above: Model Linda Evangelista in Chanel haute couture, 2003

Right: Costume designs from the show *United States of Tara* are a part of an exhibit of nominees for a 2009 Emmy Award in the category of Outstanding Television Costume Design at the Fashion Institute of Design and Merchandising (FIDM) Museum & Galleries. The title character suffers from dissociative identity disorder and each costume represents one of her personalities.

PHOTO BY TIFFANY ROSE/WIREIMAGE

75 Myths and Archetypes

According to American mythologist Joseph Campbell, exploring myths is about more than the quest for meaning. It is founded in the desire to align ourselves with experiences that resonate most with our true selves.

Fashion plays a major role in the definition of any universal archetype. When romanticizing the girl next door, what types of characteristics are attributed to her? How do virtue, wholesomeness, and purity translate into the design details and make her immediately recognizable? Her identity might be summed up by modest silhouettes that suppress her sexuality, combined with fresh, bright, happy colors and sweet details such as buttons and bows. Snap judgments may be timesavers, but there is a downside. You're left with generic, prefabricated labels with little or no depth. Who wants to run off carbon copies of someone else's ideal? The trick to using typecasting in fashion design is to do it creatively, to mix it up. What kind of fashion do you get when you shuffle the traits of the Earth mother and femme fatale? Or the damsel in distress and the trickster? In fashion, there are certainly many shades of style.

PHOTO: JOEL BENJAMIN

Tough = Leather

Soft = Ruffled Florals

76 Wit

Can funny be fashionable? It is safe to assume that Jean-Charles de Castelbajac has a sense of humor. Making clothing comical is at the heart of much of his work. Elsa Schiaparelli and Franco Moschino certainly had an appreciation for whimsy and the ridiculous. These impish designers endeavored to amuse and did not take fashion too seriously. Where is it said that a fashion designer cannot produce beautiful work that is also witty?

Fashion with a sense of humor can also make a statement. Like any good editorial cartoon, fashion can become a vehicle for delivering social or political messages. A coat made out of teddy bears might be taking a satirical stab at the ethics of using fur in fashion. The conscientious fashion designer makes a personal choice about which absurdities and abuses she might wish to poke fun at.

Humor doesn't always have to be charged with meaning. Sometimes the only motivation behind injecting couture with a little comedy is the promise of a good laugh.

PHOTO BY PIERRE VERDY/AFP/GETTY IMAGES

Above: A model wears a Lego-inspired design by French designer Jean-Charles de Castelbajac, 2008.

Right: Sebastian Errazuriz's teddy bear jacket

PHOTO: COURTESY OF SEBASTIAN ERRAZURIZ

77 Blackouts and Full Immersion

In this age of information overload, scheduling blocks of time when every channel has been turned off is essential to a designer's process—a self-imposed blackout. Downtime provides the time and space needed to edit and discard the irrelevant, making room for the next influx of data. This doesn't mean that a designer should cloister himself completely. Periods of rest can include breaking with the routine and finding alternative stimulation in unrelated and unfamiliar subjects. Recharging is well served when the creative mind is challenged in uncharted territory.

When a designer is ready to step back into the current, he can stand still and let it crash against him or he can ride the wave. The first is a "see what sticks" kind of approach—looking for creative triggers in trends that are relevant to his work. A designer who is looking to ride the wave must be ready to immerse himself.

A fashion designer also needs to find a place to test the waters, respect the environment of the industry, and stay in his league until he is prepared to play with the big boys. A designer who is dedicated will keep paddling until he feels the swell, and knows it's time to pop up and ride the wave.

Full fashion immersion

78 Representation and Abstraction

Extra! Extra! Read all about it! The written word wraps itself around fashion, literally. The direct application of text to textile allows fashion to be an instrument that conveys thoughts, phrases, and powerful messages. Designers select content to explicitly represent what they wish to express on their garments. Pages borrowed from books or newspapers, fragments of sheet music, magazine covers, or the handwritten word will speak volumes when it adorns what will be worn. The reproduction of art and photographs as textiles for fashion is a medium that gets better with technological advances. New methods allow designers to capture the minutest details. Within several collections, designer Ralph Rucci has artfully transferred both paintings of his own and photographs to fabric. Designing with images is at its best when the translation is not obvious. Figures that exceed the boundaries of the garment, becoming abstracted by their sheer scale and position, set the scene for discovery—a moment when the observer realizes there is more there than meets the eye.

Jessica Lee designs featuring a newspaper print fabric

A model wearing a gown featuring a photo print fabric by Chado Ralph Rucci, 2010

79 Symbols

The most common use of symbols in fashion to-day is the graphic T-shirt. Beyond those that are about blatant marketing, there is a tremendous market for garments in this category, which allow the wearer to express herself. Nike's "Just do it." was at the forefront of big name brands that created alternatives to the conventional wisdom of the day—slap your logo on every conceivable surface. Tag lines, meaningful messages, clever quotes, provocative images, and endearing mascots can speak to the message behind the brand better than just a logo ever could.

These carefully crafted graphics are the contemporary equivalent of a family crest, a coat of arms, or the Japanese family badges called *kamon*. Although they are all now appreciated for their beauty, each part of the design actually means something. A customer who adopts a designer's motto or symbolism is making a far greater contribution to the growth of the brand than simply making a sale. He is flying the brand's flag every time he wears it. A customer often aligns himself with these pictograms or ideograms because they are unique; there is instant recognition; they accurately represent the brand; and they often become an alternate mark or signature that embodies the message of the company as strongly as its logo does.

Phrase T: "No autographs"

Business T: Zaftigs Delicatessen

Political T: Barack Obama's presidential campaign

Destination T: Beetlebung of Martha's Vineyard

Museum T: Cooper-Hewitt National Design Museum 'Fashion in Colors' exhibit

School T: University of Kansas mascot the Jayhawk

Band T: Rolling Stones

Charity T: Marc Jacobs' for skin cancer awareness

Memorial T: Dropkick Murphys' tribute to Greg "Chickenman" Riley

Concert T: Pearl Jam Tour

Nostalgia T: Woodstock

Cause T: Yoko Ono for Fashion Against AIDS at H&M

80 Dynamics

When it comes to dance, the space that contains it can be considered a blank canvas, while the dancer who moves through it is like a brush. Each movement is similar to a brush stroke of energy across it. Keeping that in mind, a designer can virtually paint movement if he considers how his garments will become an extension of each gesture the wearer will make.

The silhouette of a skirt will change dramatically once the wearer begins to move. Will that shape restrict movement? How flexible is the fabric, and does it respond to the extension and contraction of muscle groups? Does a long hanging sleeve create the illusion of longer arms? When the hips suddenly twist, do the yards of fabric in a circular skirt whip around the body? Has the sheer volume of that skirt become an extension of the choreography? Through modern dance, choreographer Martha Graham uses the body of the dancer to pull the fabric of a garment into bold, expressive shapes.

Color is a vital part of how dynamic a movement is perceived to be. The same gesture and the same garment might suggest completely different things in different colors. A vibrant red might push the perception of power. Rendered in white it might be described in softer, gentler terms.

Texture plays a big part in how sharp or soft the movement of a garment can be. The traditional tutu is constructed to retain its rigid form while the longer "romantic tutu" is meant to be fluid. The same dance is expressed differently depending on which form is chosen.

Dance, like fashion, often reflects a certain period, culture, and tradition. The designer who understands this and also recognizes that both are nonverbal forms of communication is able to anticipate and incorporate movement into his works. The designer must also take steps to understand how much stress a garment must endure based on how people will move in it, to be sure that the materials and construction are up to the job.

Above: Classical ballet tutu at the Boston Ballet

Right: Romantic ballet tutu at the Boston Ballet

PHOTO BY SVEN DARMER/DAVIDS/WIREIMAGE

Martha Graham Dance
Company performance in
Berlin, 2008

81 Trompe L'Oeil

In some ways, fashion has always been smoke and mirrors. Every detail of fashion can be manipulated to fabricate a believable façade. With a history of misdirection, it's not surprising that fashion designers also play with perception and reality to create optical tricks for completely aesthetic reasons. Many of those illusions can be applied to the surface or woven into a textile.

Atmosphere
Aerial or atmospheric perspective is the placement and size of objects, the value of color, or the use of highlights and shadows to produce the illusion of three dimensions on a flat surface.

Convergence
Converging lines create the illusion of a shape that is diminishing into the distance.

Distortion
Sometimes called the "Café Wall" illusion, parallel lines can be distorted by outlining offset rows of black and white squares in gray.

Face
Human beings are hard-wired for face recognition, so any configuration that closely resembles the placement of facial features seems to be staring back at us.

Illusory Contour
Objects that are configured in such a way that their borders create the illusion of another shape trick the brain into imposing the perception of an object onto what is actually negative space.

Ouchi Illusion
A circle with a pattern on the cross-grain, within a square that places the same pattern on the lengthwise grain, creates the illusion that each is floating independently of the other. It is named after the Japanese op artist Hajime Ouchi.

Penrose Triangle
The impossible triangle, or the tribar, is a shape that could not exist in the real world and was inspired by the work of artist Escher.

Pointillism
Use of points of different colors that are set side by side to generate the illusion of another color was a technique used by artist Georges Seurat.

Stroop
The Stroop effect is a cognitive visual illusion that creates a conflict in the brain when the words used to identify pigments are rendered in different colors.

Stroop effect bag

Convergence

Distortion

Stroop effect

Illusory contour

Ouchi illusion

Face

Atmosphere

Pointillism

Penrose triangle

82 Space and Sculpture

Clothing can be sculpted to conform to the shape of the body or built to create abstract spaces between the garment and the wearer. When the designer sculpts to reflect the natural shape of the body it speaks to traditional European tailoring, an art form in itself when done well. This discipline relies on techniques that subdue the textile, in order to make it fit.

Less common is the exploration of how different shapes relate to the human form. This process is both conceptual and organic. The characteristics of each shape, as well as the materials, inform the designer as to how it might be manipulated independent of the body.

It can be done with every conceivable shape. One example would be the use of circles or rings. When they are applied horizontally to a design they can emulate the relationship that the rings of Saturn have to the planet itself. They completely surround the object at its center, but remain independent of the same form. Issey Miyake takes it a step further, creating a kind of kinetic sculpture. In one of his creations, alternating sizes of those rings are connected to mimic horizontal accordion pleating. The nature of structure introduces movement into the garment that seems to almost float, at times even bounce, as it skims a body in motion. Circles can also be used to create a unique three-dimensional surface treatment, as in Valentino's pink bubble sculpture.

Model wearing dress from Issey Miyake's Ready-to-Wear Collection, 1994

PHOTO BY PIERRE VERDY/AFP/GETTY IMAGES

Model wearing a pink
ensemble by haute couture
designer Valentino, 2007

83 Matters of Size: Addressing Curves

The terminology that is used to describe a woman with generous curves constitutes a reflection of how the observer perceives those proportions. By today's fashion standards, someone with a full figure, like Marilyn Monroe, would be considered fat, but would anyone really use that term to describe her? A designer might even find inspiration in the descriptors. Voluptuous might imply sensuality. Rubenesque could suggest a level of romanticism, while zaftig captures a sense of personality as well as size.

Throughout history, society has both condemned and celebrated a body of generous proportions. Theories suggest that culture, politics, and economics all play a part in what is accepted to be beautiful and in fashion. In the West African country of Mauritania, a plump figure is preferred. Gavage, or fattening, which still takes place in this region, is just as dangerous as anorexia. History shows that during times when women enjoyed greater freedoms, such as the 1920s and 1960s, feminine attributes such as the bustline and the hips were deemphasized. Economic prosperity is also thought to influence fashion norms, with thin being in during good times and bigger frames being more prevalent during challenging times.

High-profile, curvaceous celebrities continue to make strides in building an appreciation for beauty in all sizes. Queen Latifah (Dana Owens) is not only a high-profile entertainer in the music and film industries, she is also a spokesperson for Cover Girl. Emme, whose real name is Melissa Aronson, made a name for herself as a plus-size model. Her success has a direct correlation to consumers' desire to see a reflection of themselves on the runway, in print, and over the airwaves.

There are unique challenges when designing for fuller-figure women, because the structure of the clothing must fit and flow properly for comfort and movement. Foundation garments can be built into a garment to provide support while also streamlining the shape of the wearer. Linings allow the fashion fabric to skim the figure and move freely without clinging unattractively to the body. Design details can also be scaled to keep in proportion to the overall silhouette.

PHOTO BY EVAN AGOSTINI/GETTY IMAGES

Model Emme unveils the full-figured Emme Doll at FAO Schwarz in New York City, 2002.

Actress Queen Latifah arrives at the 81st Annual Academy Awards, 2009.

84 Dressing for Bowie

Is the goal of the designer to draw the observer in gently and quietly? Should the sound of fashion be somewhere in the middle, neither here nor there, just background noise? Or does the occasion call for turning up the volume in order to attract kindred spirits?

While fashion makers should be at the controls when developing the clothes, it is the consumers who will decide how loud they dare to be. Designers are advised to keep in mind that psychology is always in play when pushing the envelope, so they should be ready to address any issues with the client. In a story about her love of fashion and music, stylist and artist Nancy Hart passes on words of wisdom that a friend once shared with her about being true to your voice and your fashion sense. The essence of the message came in the form of a question. "Who are you dressing for—your bank teller or David Bowie?" The answer for her was clear: "I am dressing for Bowie!"

David Bowie is a great example of the strength of the connection between fashion and music. Through many fashion incarnations, from Ziggy Stardust to present day, he has influenced style, along the way inspiring others to express themselves. Everyone seems to have a picture in her head of who she believes she is and what she wishes to look like. Fashion provides the tools to act on creating that vision, while musicians and other high-profile figures who embrace their personal style stand as examples of how rewarding it is to do just that. A designer must ask himself, "Who and how am I looking to influence?" and "Who does my customer identify with?"

David Bowie in Wembley, London

175

85 Objects of Art

Very few artists who work with fabric compare with Christo and Jeanne-Claude. The Gates and other projects like it set the standard when it comes to art for art's sake. In addition to the rationale behind these acts of art, the daunting scale and the finite period of time in which they exist make them both one of a kind and once in a lifetime. What can the fashion designer take from this?

Most designers would be hard-pressed to make this a way of life, but engaging in the art of fashion with pure intentions can become the catalyst for a host of valuable results, including aesthetic explorations and starting dialogues with other designers.

What are the criteria for judging something a work of art? Does it elicit an emotional response? Does it challenge the observer to look at the world in a different way? Is it simply beautiful? When it comes to the art of fashion, the only conflict with the traditional definition of fine art is that a garment, no matter how extraordinary, does serve a purpose beyond just being art.

The Gates by Christo and Jeanne-Claude (1979–2005)

86 A Designer's Inheritance

It's never too early to be thinking about the future, specifically the passing on of a creative mantle—a fashion designer's last will and testament. The motivation behind such an exercise might be based in the desire to quantify the value of the brand beyond dollars and cents. It also helps to ensure that the vision will continue in the event of a transfer of power. Many companies reach a point when it becomes more lucrative to the designer to make a sale and move on, rather than remaining in charge.

Records, press clippings, and reference resources should be collected and stored by a librarian. Catalogs serve to document a designer's history of collections and special projects. Archives benefit from the curator's perspective regarding the preservation and storage of heirloom garments based on their cultural and historical significance. A brand bible will ensure consistency and preserve the integrity of the brand. The only other thing to consider is an heir apparent who would be able to take the reigns.

Designers who are not yet in a position to be thinking about this for themselves can begin to study the legacies of other designers as a source of guidance.

From Coco to Karl: The history behind the House of Chanel is one of the best examples of a successful long term legacy of fashion.

87 Luxury Washing

The concept of luxury provides three rewards, however fleeting they may be:

• A sense of power: class-driven products or encounters that build boundaries between us and them

• A sense of community: items and events that allow us to belong to a particular social group

• A sense of pleasure: goods and experiences that stimulate, indulge, and comfort

The word *luxury* is in danger of losing all meaning if you believe that every company that calls itself a luxury brand really is one. At first glance, it seems like an abuse of the term, but the definition of luxury is always subjective, especially as it pertains to fashion. Since luxury is ultimately in the eye of the beholder, many things influence our characterization of it: standard of living, supply and demand, or exceptionally distinctive.

Competing in a market saturated with claims of luxuriousness, a designer has a great advantage if she has a realistic understanding of where in the spectrum of luxury her product or service stands. This also applies to her customers. Are they aspirational? Or is luxury a baseline standard for her client? Fur, for example, is both a coveted and controversial commodity. When and how is it a necessity? Is it a symbol of a sumptuous lifestyle or of an excessive one? A clear definition of what merits the luxe label provides a kind of protection for a designer. Her claims are less at risk of being challenged if they are presented in the appropriate context.

Luxe warning: The luxury trap comes in the form of "the emperor's new clothes": blind acceptance. The nature of the fashion business is to intentionally perpetuate a cycle in which things come in and out of favor, arbitrarily increasing or decreasing the desire for them. Will the consumer, and in some cases the designer, defer to the unspoken contract between the industry, the media, and the public to agree on what luxury is at any given time? If it is generally accepted to be the standard, who will the leaders be, who will follow, and who will rebel?

Luxe costume jewelry

Viktor & Rolf fur coat, 2006

88 # Copies Degrade

The Musée de la Contrefaçon in Paris is replete with displays of counterfeit couture and every other type of faux luxury item worthy of coveting. The exhibits are curated to clearly compare the originals with the forgeries, and there is no shortage to choose from in the marketplace. At first glance, the novelty of a knockoff and the considerably lower price tag may be enticing, but these crude facsimiles don't live up to expectations.

There are a few things that consumers should consider when buying a luxury item:

- Point of sale: Is the purchase through a reputable department store or on a street corner?

- Packaging: Is it consistent with the promise of the brand?

- Price: Are you getting what you pay for?

Imitations are misrepresenting the brand, and therefore are illegal. Any product that assumes the identity of a brand is also devaluing the original work. Big companies have recourse, but the livelihood of smaller operations is threatened when their ideas are misappropriated. Cities around the world are cracking down on the purveyors of false fashions, confiscating and destroying them. Reflecting on which materials, techniques, and finishing touches are incorporated into a design will help to make the design harder to duplicate, resulting in a product that is not profitable to duplicate.

Genuine and counterfeit bags are displayed at the Musée de la Contrefaçon in Paris. The museum serves to highlight the impact that fake items have both on the producers of authentic products in regard to consumers and the wider economy, and on general health and safety issues.

89 Platforms

To be prepared when opportunity knocks, a designer should always be building a platform with and around his work. Authentic experiences and valuable exchanges are a big part of cultivating a loyal fan base. High-caliber connections put the designer in a position to energize and activate that audience when needed.

Before embarking on the development of a complicated communication network, choices need to be made regarding which outlets best align with the goals of the designer: a website, social media, project partnerships, blogs, live events, television appearances, relevant products, writing books, authored magazine articles, speaking engagements, work experience, and teaching opportunities. The designer should also establish and prioritize his values, because shared ideals forge strong bonds between him and his constituents. These systems allow the fashion designer to add value by encouraging interactivity; involving his audience through regular updates, mobilizing the masses with calls to action, rewarding loyalty, and extending the personality of the brand.

Isaac Mizrahi presents *The Adventures of Sandee the Supermodel.* 1997 S&S Editions Comic Book Series. Artwork by William Frawley

How to Have Style by Isaac Mizrahi, 2008

Isaac Mizrahi uses a segment called "Sketches & Answers" to sketch out answers to audience questions about style.

Unzipped DVD of 1995 documentary by Douglas Keeve

Business Week magazine dubbed Isaac Mizrahi a "one-man brand," which describes his exceptional talent for translating his vision and style across a wide variety of platforms. In addition to a documentary, a series of comic books, and a book on personal style, he designed a diffusion collection for Target; served as creative director for Liz Claiborne; designs products for QVC; hosts reality show, *The Fashion Show*, on Bravo TV; communicates with fans via a daily video-blog, Facebook, and Twitter; hosts the web-show, WATCHISAAC.com; and was among the first generation of designers to livestream his fashion runway shows online. He was also the costume designer for stage revivals of *The Women* (2001), *Barefoot in the Park* (2006), the operetta, *Three Penny Opera* (2006), and the Metropolitan Opera's production of *Orfeo ed Euridice* (2008).

90 Label Maker

Part of the fashion design process involves how information about the garments you create will be shared with your customer. There are laws regarding how clothing must be labeled. In the United States, the Federal Trade Commission requires that most textile and wool products clearly identify fiber content, country of origin, and brand or manufacturer, and that those labels be securely fastened. They can be sewn in or ironed on. A label printed directly onto the garment can end up as part of the design. The percentages of fiber content for each component of the garment—body, lining, interlining, and/or decoration—must also be included. Keeping tabs on information is the designer's responsibility.

Care labels for apparel should provide complete instructions regarding care and any warning specific to that garment to ensure that the quality is not compromised. Warnings should use clear terminology, such as "Do not iron," "No bleach," and "Dry clean only." A system of universal symbols for virtually every contingency is also available.

Designer name labels, hang tags, and price tickets are usually designed to be extensions of the brand.

Universal Garment-Care Symbols

WASHING

Machine Wash Cycles

 Normal

 Permanent Press

 Delicate Gentle

 Hand Wash

 Do Not Wash

Water Temperature

 Cold (86°F [30°C])

 Warm (104°F [40°C])

 Hot (122°F [50°C])

 Do Not Ring

BLEACHING

 Any Bleach When Needed

 Only Non-Chlorine Bleach When Needed

 Do Not Bleach

DRYING

Tumble Dry Cycles

Normal	Permanent Press	Delicate/ Gentle	Line Dry	Drip Dry	Dry Flat

Tumble Drying Temperatures

Any Heat	High Heat	Medium Heat	Low Heat	No Heat/Air	Do Not Tumble Dry

---

IRONING

Iron Dry or Steam

Low (230°F [110°C])	High (392°F [200°C])	Do Not Iron

Medium (302°F [150°C])	No Steam

DRY CLEANING

Dry Clean	Do Not Dry Clean

91 Master and Apprentice

Master, apprentice; instructor, student; mentor, protégé: The semantics here are not as important as the acts of giving and receiving that take place when the inexperienced benefit from those who have come before. Donna Karan started working under Anne Klein in 1970. In 1974, when Klein passed away, Karan joined forces with Louis Dell'Olio to continue to build on the Anne Klein legacy. This partnership continued until 1984, when Karan left to begin her solo career. After the untimely death of her brother, Gianni Versace, in 1997, Donatella Versace was able to step in and move forward with his vision for Versace. Her experience and respect for the brand allowed her to honor the position the company had earned in the fashion world, and still project her vision for the future of the label.

Yohji Yamamoto's daughter, Limi Yamamoto, was exposed to fashion early in life. She carries on her father's passion for design through her work, a label called Limi Feu. She had shown in Tokyo for several years before a successful Paris debut in 2007. Her father's aesthetic can certainly be felt throughout her work, but the second-generation Yamamoto has an independent perspective on fashion all her own.

Not only have these relationships benefited the "master's" brand, in that the apprentice can maintain the designer's vision of the brand, but they also allow the apprentice the chance to instill her own sensibilities in the fashion. It's a win-win situation.

PHOTO BY DMI/TIME & LIFE PICTURES/GETTY IMAGES

Fashion designers/siblings
Gianni and Donatella
Versace, 1990

A model wearing an ensemble from the Limi Feu fashion show, 2010

92 Designing the Job

"Create a job you love, and you will never have to work a day in your life": It's a slightly modified version of the wisdom of Confucius. Designing your own job may sound like a luxury, or perhaps is the very definition of a fantasy, but in spite of how unrealistic it sounds, there are some pretty simple steps you can take to get a little bit closer to that ideal work experience. The good news is that a fashion designer is already on the artist's path, so making an emotional investment in her work is par for the course.

First, no one wants to hear, "That's not my job." If something needs to be done, someone who sincerely cares about the end result also cares about how to get there, so she assigns herself tasks that seem petty. This means there are no small jobs.

Second, "I was only following orders" is just as bad. Have a point of view, and let your voice be heard. Risk and sacrifice come with the territory if innovation is going to take place. Every time you suppress yourself and avoid uncomfortable situations you devalue yourself and your work.

Finally, this is not the domain of a select few. Having purposeful pursuits, and letting your work ethic classify you as indispensable, is the currency you need to remain competitive. Going the extra mile will pay off in the end.

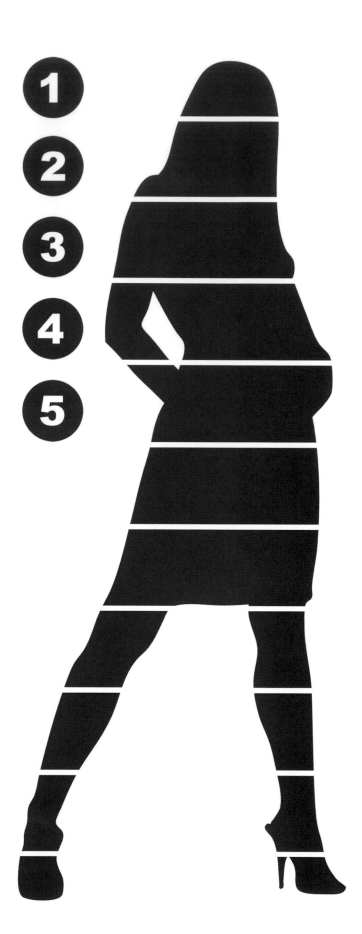

The top ten things to consider when designing your ultimate job: Ask yourself how does this job meet your expectations with regard to: 1) creativity; 2) financial compensation; 3) recognition; 4) community involvement; 5) productive teamwork; 6) strong leadership; 7) opportunity for advancement; 8) skill development and continuing education; 9) environmental impact; 10) intellectual integrity.

6

7

8

9

10

93 External Influences

Individuals and organizations that have the authority to make their views known to a broad audience can have a profound effect on public opinion, and ultimately the commercial success of a designer. A nod of approval from a respected industry professional can fuel the fire while a negative gesture may have the power to extinguish it.

Christian Bérard, known as Bébé, was an artist in Paris who had great influence in the 1930s and 1940s. He was sought after by clients of haute couturiers because his fashion assessments held a lot of weight. In many ways, he was a predecessor to the stylist. Stylists provide a valuable service because they process fashion information in a way that takes into consideration the needs of the client, the vision of the designer, and the environment in which the work will be seen.

As long as there are creative individuals who are brave enough to share their work with the rest of the world, there will be critics. Anyone who is pursuing a career in fashion is familiar with *Vogue*'s editor-in-chief, Anna Wintour. It is important to remember that she had established her reputation long before movies and books made her a household name. Years of experience are responsible for her immeasurable impact on the careers of designers and the fashion industry as a whole.

Whether the source of influence is international, national, regional, or local, there will be journalists, editors, and stylists who help guide the direction for fashion under their watch. On the global stage, Grace Coddington, Hamish Bowles, and Andre Leon Talley are just a handful of fashion editors who are held in high regard for how well they are able to interpret fashion. These arbiters of taste enjoy a broader understanding of the fashion landscape and, as a result, are in a position to share invaluable feedback. Although designers should always trust their instincts, they would be well advised to listen when the criticism is constructive.

PHOTO BY EUGENE GOLOGURSKY/WIREIMAGE

Grace Coddington and Hamish Bowles attend a Marc by Marc Jacobs fashion show, 2010.

Andre Leon Talley

94 Lifestyle: A Rosetta Stone

The designer discovers or creates his unique Rosetta stone, a primer that helps him to decode and translate the intricacies of other fields. Armed with a key, he approaches his design challenge as an interpreter. Although he needs to work within the natural boundaries of his craft, he can introduce his audiences to new things, educating them as to how viable and valuable they are within the framework of fashion.

Whether it's pop culture or science and technology, gaining insights into other areas stimulates the design process and spawns new ideas.

The arts have always stimulated the creative mind, but dedicated practice of another art form—whether it is painting or performance—gains admission into a new dimension of that artistic outlet. Analyzing horticulture and the culinary arts provides insight into how to cultivate plant life and prepare food. Animal, insect, and sea life also broaden the scope of understanding of how things work. Even if in-depth comprehension is not the goal, a casual acquaintance with the subject can be enough to trigger an idea if the designer is open to it.

Fashion and art:
preschool masterpiece by
Zak Atkinson as inspiration

Fashion and technology:
circuit board surface as decoration

Fashion and architecture:
reflecting patterns in man-made structures

Fashion and food:
produce provides a source of silhouette and color

Fashion and transportation:
emulating the finish and flair of automobiles

Fashion and nature:
identifying layers of texture in landscapes

Fashion and lifestyle:
beach toys provide common reference points

95 Fashion Portals

There is little point to all the hard work involved in fashion design if the final product doesn't go anywhere. Designers must also design systems that distribute their work to many different destinations, utilizing lots of channels—with each channel having a distinct message.

In-store, it is all about hanger appeal. Retailers expect the product to be packaged in a way that maintains the integrity of the design.

Screen appeal rules online, and that means beautiful, clear images. The e-commerce experience falls short in many ways because there is no way to touch the fabric or try on the garment. A picture must provide a great deal of visual information and be strong enough to engage the customer.

A showroom is a bridge between designer and buyer. The sales representative must be informed and invested in the product because she is educating and stimulating the client in order to make the sale.

Celebrity association is one of the easiest ways to scale up perceived importance when the delivery channel is through imagery—either motion or still shots. Having a well-known persona representing the product is an asset.

Pop-up stores, taking a collection on tour, trunk shows, and private shopping experiences are just a few of the guerilla tactics that can be employed to surprise and seduce the shopper.

Fashion shows and shopping events put the clothes on display within the context of entertainment. The runway presentation is transformed with theatrical models, hair, makeup, and styling.

It's important to compartmentalize different needs for the press and what they ultimately need to deliver to their audiences, as well: A blogger is looking to express his opinion; the journalist needs to present the facts; an editor needs to place the designer's work within the context of the current vision for the market. How can you help each of them reach their goals?

Last, and most important, public opinion and word of mouth are paramount. Public opinion, in particular, is a powerful conveyor of messages. It also validates and perpetuates a designer's reputation.

PHOTO: LOUIS SELVITELLA

The fashion show: *Girls Rule!* Runway fashion show at Bryant Park during New York Fashion Week

The pop-up store: Puma transformed shipping containers into prefabricated retail stores that can literally pop up anywhere.

96 Diversification and Specialization

Find one thing you do well, and do just that. Whether the niche is bridalwear or skiwear, the path to specialization is one which requires that a designer focus exclusively on a particular market and master the design intricacies unique to that field.

Find one thing you do well, and translate what was successful about it into many different products. During the late 1800s, Burberry established itself by focusing on outdoor attire. The company is also credited with the invention of gabardine, a durable, breathable, water-resistant fabric. At the start of World War I, the company was commissioned to develop what ended up being the trench coat. Its signature tartan was introduced during the 1920s as a lining for the coat.

The symbols of the brand are interpreted and adapted to the needs and desires of today's consumer. Outerwear is still at the heart of the brand, but items such as the iconic trench coat are reimagined each season. The classic black, tan, and red Burberry pattern, now a registered trademark, is no longer relegated to linings. It can be found on apparel, fragrances, accessories, luggage, and even swimwear.

There is an argument to be made for both sides, but diversification definitely benefits from the prestige of having done one thing well for a long time. Good foundations provide an excellent environment for experimentation and expansion.

Right: Bridal gown

Below: Skiwear ensemble by M. Miller

PHOTO: JOEL BENJAMIN

PHOTO: JOEL BENJAMIN

A model displays a swimsuit ensemble by Burberry, 2005.

97 Crowdsourcing Style

Too many cooks in the kitchen spoil the soup, and too many opinions during the design process can turn out diluted or incoherent work. Herd behavior often strives to appeal to the lowest common denominator. Being well aware of the downside of design by committee is a good reason for creating a filter for feedback and criticism, constructive or otherwise.

The flip side of this is the positive power of the people. Crowdsourcing is reaching out to broad audiences—most commonly over the Internet—to help develop designs, raise money, and mobilize people. Services such as Kickstarter.com help volunteer organizations, charities, startups, designers, and bands level the playing field between amateurs and professionals. They remove the middleman, allowing a designer to go directly to the customer for content, funding, and distribution. The goals of crowdsourcing include finding resources, outsourcing projects, finding funding, courting inspiration, gaining a democratic consensus, minimizing costs, and taking advantage of the wisdom of the masses. When it is managed well, mass collaboration can be leveraged to take advantage of having multiple designers participating in problem solving, multiple sources contributing components of the design, and finding scores of patrons who will support a designer's vision.

Making a good pitch online is not much different from the process of drafting a business plan to impress a banker. A compelling case must be made, because investors of any kind are looking for sound ideas as well as a spark—not to mention a reward for getting involved. Taking advantage of this platform raises awareness and helps to gauge what people actually want, and potentially empowers participants to become a community of brand citizens.

Above: Designer Valerie Mayen of *Project Runway* fame, used Kickstarter.com successfully to raise funds for a startup venture. The project is a fashion design incubator called Buzz & Growl, based in Cleveland, Ohio.

98 Labors of Love: DIY

It's easy to say "I could have done that." As any designer knows, setting aside the time, getting organized, and figuring out exactly how to do that is another thing altogether. Satisfaction is cited as the primary motivation for doing it yourself, which explains why so many invest time and money in classes, workshops, books, magazines, and kits that allow them to literally take matters into their own hands.

Writing off homespun attempts at fashion as merely crafts and hokey hobbies is a mistake. Although the results may display an obvious lack of training, great ingenuity and a wealth of rough concepts often can be polished in the hands of a trained designer. Many things produced in this environment cater to unidentified niche markets that might have otherwise gone unnoticed by designers. The influence of these micromarkets should not be underestimated. Natural talents with the potential to transform a pastime into a career now have distribution channels such as Etsy.com and public markets in which artisans and aspiring designers can show and sell their work. Pay attention to trends in these markets.

Etsy success story: Moop, a Pittsburgh–based company that designs and manufactures handmade bags, was able to use the website to build their business. Owner/designer Wendy Downs describes Etsy.com as a place she could experiment with and learn how to run a business.

99 Rapid Prototyping: Twenty-Four-Hour Fashion

Reality shows such as *Project Runway* and projects such as the 24-Hour Filmmaking Festival are good examples of popular "sink or swim" enterprises. Be warned, however, that condensing the time allowed for a project to be executed can produce both brilliant and disastrous results. As entertainment, it might be fun to observe the praise and the pitfalls, but in the real world, this could correlate to the beginning or end of a career. Working in the fashion industry doesn't always mean running at breakneck speeds, but it does demand that creatives be able to make smart decisions in crisis mode.

Not everyone is cut out for it, so it's important to impose time-sensitive challenges to test for vulnerabilities. These are great opportunities to learn how to anticipate and avoid the kinds of things that have the potential to derail the design process. Situations in which speed impedes the process and threatens to thwart creativity are ideal occasions in which to consider the skills that still need to be honed; immediate situation assessment, quick decision making, efficient application of techniques, fast problem solving, and/or creative resourcefulness.

Some designers thrive on the stress of tight, and sometimes unrealistic, deadlines. Rapid-fire fashion design relies heavily on instinct and experience. Beyond crossing the finish line, success under these conditions should also be measured by how well executed the work is, and how clearly the designer's vision is perceived. Speed as a catalyst for good design is a difficult thing to sustain. The rush of these pressure-cooker projects may provide an addictive rush of adrenaline, but that is hard to rely on.

(uni)forms are designer/artist Ying Gao's response to the phrase "Speed kills creativity." By using morphing software, she was able to generate new uniform designs based on the original within seconds.

PHOTOS BY DOMINIQUE LAFOND

Original 1940s German female worker's uniform

Ying Gao (uni)form #1

Ying Gao (uni)form #2

Ying Gao (uni)form #3

Ying Gao (uni)form #4

Ying Gao (uni)form #5

Ying Gao (uni)form #6

100 What Is Good Fashion?

Assigning value to something that stems from individual creativity is a very subjective thing when the only criteria are the standards of the day. In addition to being judged for its aesthetic value, fashion is also charged with being functional. In hindsight, it is easy to assess why some houses endure, some make a brief but significant mark at a singular point in time, and some fade from memory. The third group, although it demands greater effort, has the potential to reward us with exciting discoveries. For instance, not many people know that architect Frank Lloyd Wright designed dresses for his wife and for a select few of the ladies he created homes for. So, what type of designer produces good, if not great, fashion?

The inventors, who introduce unprecedented ideas—necessity often fuels these designers, as they approach a design challenge using alternative methods. The architects, who design the buildings we inhabit—they will also look to create a lifestyle around their vision to achieve a comprehensive unity. The scholars, who are the standard-bearers, serving and protecting the art and craft of fashion—they immerse themselves in the minutia of how others throughout history have done it, and as a result, they keep those practices alive. Without these stewards of fashion, every generation of designers would be starting from scratch. And finally, the rebels—whether we understand them or not we appreciate the iconoclasts because they have an impact on our lives. Their imagination and passion for the work is fueled by an unyielding need to provoke and challenge us. Alexander McQueen was one of those bad boys of fashion who was known for being true to his vision. He will be remembered for the power and purity of his work. In the end, one word defines good fashion. Integrity.

A model wearing a gown from Alexander McQueen's last collection during the 2010 CFDA Fashion Awards at Alice Tully Hall at Lincoln Center, 2010

1. **Alyce Santoro**
www.alycesantoro.com

2. **Berber Soepboer & Michiel Schuurman**
www.berbersoepboer.nl

3. **Blauer Uniforms**
www.blauer.com

4. **Bob Packert**
www.packertphotography.com

5. **Boston Ballet**
www.bostonballet.org

6. **Cory Stierley**
www.csphotographic.com

7. **Daniel Faucher Couture**
www.danielfauchercouture.com

8. **Dominique Lafond**
www.dominiquelafond.com

9. **Fine Art by T**
fineartbyt@yahoo.com

10. **Goods of Conscience**
www.goodsofconscience.com

11. **Isaac Mizrahi**
www.isaacmizrahiny.com

12. **Jessica Weiser**
www.jessicaweiser.com

13. **Joel Benjamin**
www.joelbenjamin.com

14. **Karolina Zmarlak**
www.karolinazmarlak.com

15. **Kevin Day**
www.kevindayphotography.com

16. **Lucy Orta**
www.studio-orta.com

17. **Marie-Eve Tremblay**
m.evetremblay@hotmail.com

18. **Massachusetts College of Art and Design**
www.massart.edu

19. **Moop**
www.moopshop.com
www.etsy.com/shop/moop

20. **Oscar Correcher**
www.oscarcorrecherphotography
.blogspot.com

21. **Philips Design, SKIN Probe Project**
www.design.philips.com/probes/projects
/dresses/index.page

22. **Poor Little Rich Girl**
www.shoppoorlittlerichgirl.com

23. **School of Fashion Design, Boston**
www.schooloffashiondesign.org

24. **Sebastian Errazuriz**
www.meetsebastian.com

25. **Simplynate Photography**
www.simplynate.com

26. **Tracy Aiguier**
www.tracyaiguier.com

27. **Uniform Project**
www.theuniformproject.com

28. **Valerie Mayen Buzz & Growl**
www.buzzandgrowl.com
www.kickstarter.com/projects/yellowcake/
buzz-and-growl-clevelands-new-fashion-
incubator

29. **Victoria Dominguez-Bagu**
mariavictoriadesigns@gmail.com

30. **Ying Gao**
www.cavaaller.blogspot.com

Special thanks to

Robert Frye, Viola Gonzalez, Tina Calderin, Jake & Ena Calderin,

Patricia & Wallace Frye, Kilsy Curiel, Rafael Villalona, Kathy Pilarski,

Richard Brooks, Mary Garthe, Jacobo & Edith Calderin,

Fructuoso & Gloria Gonzalez, Carmen Rita Gonzalez, Rebecca Gonzalez,

Jennifer Hudson, Jaycey Wetherington, Jaclyn McGeehan, Jamie Mendoza,

Doreen Mendez, Alicia Kennedy, Betsy Gammons, Roytel Montero, Rosina Rucci,

Cheryl Richardson, James Hannon, Sondra Grace, Richard Bath, Joel Benjamin,

Bob Packert, Victoria Domiguez-Bagu, Marie-Eve Tremblay, Lisa Baker,

Tracy Aiguier, Jane Conway-Caspe, Jayne Avery, Dana Moscardelli, Terri Mahn,

Daniel Faucher, Lisa Taranto, Elaina Barisano, Lisa Micheels, Phyllis Misité

Louis Selvitella, Meredith Byam-Miller, Nancy Hart, Mariclaire Hession-Landman,

Laura, Harrison & Amanda Soelter, Bethany VanDelft, Munjeet Geyer,

Alex, Cynthia & Zak Atkinson, Mark Bailey, Tony Halston, Donna Rice,

Chuck Lacombe, Wendy Downs, Valerie Mayen, Rachel Kacenjar,

Marie Galvin, Shaunt Sarian, Jennifer Lurie, Erika Stair, Sarah Carnabuci,

Amie Belobrow, Shinroku Ohashi, Lisa Koplow Nogler,

Joe Carl, Shannon Glasheen, Jeff Lahens, Shelley Chhabra,

Mariel MacNaughton, Charles Heightchew,

Ying Gao, Father Andrew O'Connor, and Lisa Koenigsberg

Thank you to faculty, administration, and students past and present

at the School of Fashion Design in Boston.

PHOTO: TRACY AIGUIER

Jay Calderin was born and raised in New York City. The *Los Angeles Times* called his first book, *Form, Fit, and Fashion*, "a new fashion bible for designers, aspirers, and the just plain curious; this tome contains all the secrets." After moving to Boston and discovering the great wealth of local fashion talent, he adopted the city as his new home, where he founded and became the executive director of Boston Fashion Week.

He is an instructor and the director of creative marketing at the School of Fashion Design in Boston, a position that allows him to be involved in programming development and community outreach, while also functioning as an industry liaison. In addition to the wide variety of fashion and professional development courses he teaches at SFD, he has also served as an instructor at the Massachusetts College of Art and Design, Burdett College, and Lasell College. His pursuits as a professional coach and motivational speaker have afforded him opportunities to share his ideas about the art and industry of fashion at institutions including Harvard University, Wellesley College, Tufts University, Lesley University, Babson College, Museum of Fine Arts Boston, Peabody Essex Museum, Boston Public Library, and the *Hatch* Festival in Bozeman, Montana.

In his capacity as a fashion designer his work has graced the pages of *Vogue, Elle*, the *Boston Globe* and the *Boston Globe Sunday Magazine*. He has authored numerous articles and columns for newspapers, magazines, and the Internet. He has worked as an accredited fashion editor, photographer, and as a fashion commentator for television. He credits his solid foundation in fashion to his training at the High School of Fashion Industries in New York City. The school cultivated a work ethic and allegiance to excellence that has served him well ever since. Throughout his career he has maintained a passionate dedication to the importance of giving back to the community. As an extension of that commitment, he works with local charities as well as grassroots endeavors to nurture and develop new talent—a driving force behind his work with the Fashion Group International as a regional director in Boston.

See his website at www.calderin3.com.